The Yoga of Consciousness

From Waking, Dream and Deep Sleep to Self-realization

David Frawley
(Vamadeva Shastri)

All illustrations, line drawings and cover
by U. Mahesh Prabhu
www.vedic-management.com, www.vivaswaan.com

First Edition, 2020

ISBN: 978-1-6086-9238-5

Library of Congress Control Number: 2019954718

Published by:
Lotus Press,
P.O. Box 325, Twin Lakes, Wisconsin 53181 USA
www.lotuspress.com
lotuspress@lotuspress.com
800-824-6396

Table Of Contents

Part IV - Exploring Deeper in Traditional Teachings

Part V - Appendices

Foreword by Yogini Shambhavi

We live in a magical universe that transcends all boundaries and limitations, appearances and measurements – for which time and space, name and form are but mere masks and mirrors. We knew this mysterious fact of our greater cosmic existence when we were children, when every place and moment was an opportunity for play, fearless exploration and delight. Yet we lost this depth as we grew up in the outer world to eventually be taken in by social identities and material needs as our true work and purpose in life, forgetting our blissful origins and spontaneous expression.

We can still return to that primordial magic of awareness if we learn how the light of Consciousness moves through us every day and can transport us beyond all sorrow. Each day can be a new awakening to our deathless reality that embraces the whole of nature down to the very ground on which we stand. Every new thing we see glimmering in the wind can be an awakening to our greater Self that is one with all, as the space within space, the time beyond time.

There are dreams within our dreams veiled in mystery that can take us beyond all desire, if we pursue the deepest wishes and prayers of the heart, which is to embrace the entire universe within us like the flow of the river.

There is an eternal peace at the core of our being in which is the ultimate state of rest, renewal, surrender and transcendence – where no thought can enter, the calm depth of the cosmic night of boundless awareness.

Yoga Shakti

The light of consciousness is our true Self and being, the presence of Lord Shiva, the immortal awareness within us. The energy of Consciousness is the very Shakti or energy of our lives as well as the universal breath. This Shakti force allows us to aspire to transcend our mortal being raising itself in its prayer for eternity.

The energy of Consciousness is the Yoga Shakti or power of Yoga, through which alone inner transformation can be an enduring reality, not a passing glimmer.

The Goddess is the power of Consciousness, Chit-Shakti, from which all creativity arises from the infinite, like overflowing ocean waves. We can discover her beauty and grace at each moment that we become aware of the movement of life as our own inner effulgence beyond all expectations.

That inner power of consciousness, our own inner Yoga Shakti, takes us from waking to dream and deep sleep and back again every day. It holds the movement of our lives through birth and death, joy and sorrow, light and dark. It contains every possibility of growth, evolution and transformation. The Yoga Shakti holds the three changing outer states of waking, dream and deep sleep in the embrace of Turiya, the transcendent fourth that is timeless and eternal, such as the Upanishads proclaim.

Only when we understand this daily sacred movement in

awareness do we truly know ourselves or our place in the vast cosmos. Yet we seldom take the time or the effort to turn within and let the universe express itself through us.

Instead of using our consciousness and its power of seeing (drigshakti) to find beauty and bliss everywhere, we get trapped in our human minds, with their memories, expectations and demands, and all the compulsions that arise from them in our human activities that drive us day by day. Our ego rears its contrary head and gets us caught on the treadmill of desire and fear, wanting to become something transient for the sake of others, rather than remain in the immortal essence of our being dependent upon no one.

Certainly our five senses present us with numerous wonders of sound, touch, sight, taste and smell that we can explore endlessly in various permutations and combinations throughout our lives. Yet we have corresponding inner senses through which we can contact inner realms of music, light and vibration far more entrancing than the physical world. At the deepest level is the inner eye of Seeing, in which we become whatever we see and the light of Boundless awareness and wonder embraces all.

The Yoga of Consciousness

Vamadeva's book, the *Yoga of Consciousness* is an experiential exploration of the wonders of Consciousness and its daily unfoldment in a comprehensive and systematic manner. In it Vamadeva unfolds the essence of Yoga and Vedanta echoing great Vedic sages like Vishvamitra and Parashara, with their worship of the eternally wakeful cosmic fire within us, and Advaitic gurus like Adi Shankara and Ramana Maharshi who take us directly to the Self that transcends birth and death.

The book asks many profound questions but shows how we

can discover the answers by simply observing our own daily movement in consciousness from waking to sleep with an inner opening to the reality of light behind the senses. The *Yoga of Consciousness* shows us the universal reality of Yoga as the unity and oneness behind all the brilliant diversity and endless expansion of all that we see.

The spiritual heart (hridaya) is the basis of experience and reality for all creatures. It's light is reflected through the mind into an outer effulgence that forms the external world. The mind then diversifies through the five senses. Yet all of this is but the vibration of our own being, the Yoga Shakti, the Spanda or resurgent wave of truth, auspiciousness and beauty, Satyam, Shivam, Sundaram.

We can attune ourselves to this movement of delight at any moment we are willing to fully focus upon it and let go of the distractions of the mind. Such wonders are there at every moment that we direct our gaze with an inner intent, willing to contemplate with ecstasy, not merely observe for personal gain.

Of course, this inner effulgence is very far from us in the media world today, in which we are trapped in media boxes and screens that have become our reality and state of awareness programmed from the outside. Yet it is present in every breath, heartbeat and twinkling of the eye, if we are willing to surrender within and let go of our outer turbulence and demands.

When perusing his book on consciousness, Vamadeva's request to write the foreword to such a masterful piece of inner work took me by complete surprise. It is in deep reverence and gratitude to his flow of divine grace in my life that I express my thoughts here. No doubt it will take me several lifetimes to experience the nectar of his wisdom.

Vamadeva

Vamadeva Shastri is a living Yogi in the soul of an ancient Rishi, sharing his deeper knowledge with the world of seekers in its simplicity, authenticity and clarity. He is a gentle humble being walking his expression both written and spoken in his everyday existence.

My most touching moment was when Sri K. Natesan, a great disciple of Bhagavan Ramana Maharshi, took my hand in his frail clasp, yet looking at Vamadeva whispered, "Nayana, Nayana" (a special name for Ganapati Muni). I was not aware of Sri Natesan's great devotion to Kavyakantha Ganapati Muni. Only later meditating on Ganapati Muni did I see a deepening resemblance of Vamadeva's features and his great passion for Devi expressed through his own spoken and written expression.

My fervent prayer has been one of implicit devotion and conscious surrender to the Mother Goddess experiencing Her wisdom as life's experience. Lord Shiva who drew me to his Devi in the form of Kali as She watched my footsteps guiding me to work consciously and truthfully through my own karmic journey.

The *Yoga of Consciousness* helps us return to our cosmic journey through realms of vision of which our current human life is but an episode veiled in higher motivations that we might not truly understand.

My prayer is please do not just read this book but contemplate its deeper meaning throughout the rhythms of your day. It is not a theoretic book, nor does it promote any idea or dogma. It is a mirror of our daily reality whose cosmic connections we forget.

May we be inspired to imagine all higher possibilities when we dream, and to return to our enduring inner peace when asleep at night. Let us learn to aspire to the infinite as we move through the deep sleep state into the forays of a conscious dawn every morning. We hold all time and space within us in our own daily journey in Consciousness. Let us remember our true pilgrimage from darkness to light, from time to the eternal.

Yogini Shambhavi

Santa Fe, New Mexico
December 2019

Author's Preface

The *Yoga of Consciousness* examines how our consciousness, identity and prana change through waking, dream and deep sleep – and more importantly how we can follow this process to higher levels of awareness behind the ordinary human state. The book proposes specific yogic insights and approaches to take us beyond these three ordinary states to the transcendent state of pure unity consciousness beyond both body and mind.

In this research, I have followed the views of traditional Yoga and Vedantic texts like the *Yoga Sutras* and *Upanishads*. Notably it focuses on the teaching of the *Mandukya Upanishad,* which explains the mystery of Om and guides us to the state of transcendence. The book does not focus on the physical ramifications of waking and sleep, but on how to use these ordinary states of mind to move beyond a physical and outer view of reality altogether.

The *Yoga of Consciousness* rests upon teachings that I have learned from Vedantic gurus, texts and traditions. These include the teachings of Bhagavan Ramana Maharshi, Kavyakantha Ganapati Muni, Swami Rama Tirtha, Adi Shankara, and Sadguru Sivananda Murty.

The *Yoga of Consciousness* covers some of the same ground as popular approaches to Yoga Nidra today, and can serve as an expansion of that teaching. Yet its purpose is deeper than most of what is called Yoga Nidra, aiming to deconstruct our sense of physical reality so that we can experience the reality of Pure Consciousness. It includes Yoga Nidra as part of a greater approach to Self-realization going beyond body and mind. It is not aiming at Yoga Nidra as a technique of relaxation or better sleep, which does have its preliminary value. The book aims to take the reader beyond Yoga Nidra in the personal and physical sense to Yoga Nidra as an experience of cosmic consciousness, the universal sleep of mergence into the Supreme Self.

My purpose is also not to explain what modern science says about the brain and the sleep process, except peripherally, though this can be very interesting. It is to examine the ancient yogic wisdom that can take us far beyond the boundaries of science as it is today. Yogic knowledge does not accept the physical world as ultimately real or the bodily ego as our true identity. It recognizes a deeper level of energy and intelligence underlying both our human nature and the universe as whole, extending to a cosmic intelligence and unitary awareness beyond all limitation or qualification.

Relative to my previous titles, the *Yoga of Consciousness* continues with the issues discussed in my earlier books *Vedantic Meditation, Ayurveda and the Mind, Inner Tantric Yoga* and *Shiva, the Lord of Yoga*, among several others.

The book provides keys to develop a deeper awareness on the part of the reader, so that instead of merely sleeping at night one can move into an enduring state of meditative inquiry. The book is not meant simply to provide information but to facilitate a change in consciousness. It is addressed to your inner being that transcends body and mind not just to the human self or personal intellect bound by illusion and duality.

For Sanskrit terms we have accepted as is terms like Purusha or karma that have entered into the existing literature. We have included transliterated Sanskrit for key phrases and mantras for those who know that, and a Sanskrit key in the back.

I would like to specially thank *Hinduism Today* magazine for their enthusiasm about the theme and for presenting a special feature based upon the book, which was then a work in progress, in its April-May-June 2017 edition.

For editing of the book, Dr. Narasimha B. Bhat was most helpful and Yogi Baba Prem. We must specially thank U. Mahesh Prabhu for his comments and, most importantly, for his wonderful illustrations and extraordinary cover.

May everyone awaken to his or her eternal Being, boundless Consciousness and unqualified bliss! But for this to occur we must cross over the dark unknowing of deep sleep and return to our nature as pure Light. Let every day for us be a journey into unbounded awareness.

Dr. David Frawley (Pandit Vamadeva Shastri)

Santa Fe, New Mexico
January 2020

Introductory Note by Hinduism Today

Hinduism Today magazine has a forty year love affair with how India's ancient yogis understood such things as memory, identity, astrology, hatha yoga, health and such. Over the years we have collaborated with Vamadeva Shastri on these topics, so when in 2017 we set out to cover the topic of sleep, we turned to him. The article he did for our readers was a rare exploration of sleep and its related states of mind.

Acharya Vamadeva has crafted from that summary a complete book, The Yoga of Consciousness, in which he unpacks the elements in his usual articulate and penetrating way. If ever you wanted to truly comprehend the four states of consciousness, and what lies beyond, this is the map for your path forward.

Paramacharya Sadasivanatha Swami
Hinduism Today Magazine

Part I

Foundations of the Yoga of Consciousness

Introduction: Author's Experience and Inspiration

Our lives, if we look deeply, consist of a journey in consciousness at various levels from waking to sleep to birth and death. All of our experiences take place much like images reflected in the mirror of consciousness that extends through all space and time.

This inner journey can be a great adventure in awareness leading to boundless wisdom and enduring bliss beyond time and space. It holds the potential for the highest and most enduring peace and happiness. Yet, because we do not look deeply, we experience life as a mere series of events in the external world, with all of its uncertainty, duality and turbulence.

We easily miss this background profound awareness and get lost in the detailed movement of outer phenomena perceived through the physical senses. We forget that the drama of human life happens within the field of a vaster cosmic reality, and that our ultimate purpose lies beyond the transient concerns of mere physical existence.

In a conditioned fixation on the external world, we neglect to observe more consequential movements in our own minds and hearts. Merely seeking more detailed information or better skills about the outer world cannot take us beyond darkness and sorrow; for that higher task, we need to develop a direct awareness. This is not beyond our capacity but requires a radical shift in how we view ourselves and of the world that we are part of.

Our lives comprise not just an outer journey using the physical body and its limited senses; our lives also follow an inner journey through different domains of awareness. These include our daily states of consciousness as waking, dream and deep sleep, but can extend to higher states of awareness beyond the material world. Our physical life is more only a shadow than our true place in the universal existence.

Our inner movement in awareness consists of more than emotional responses to the outer environment, or the mind's efforts to figure out how the external world operates. Our deeper internal journey takes us beyond the world, which means ultimately beyond body and mind, time and space altogether. In fact, we are happiest when we forget the world, forget ourselves and touch a timeless inspiration that connects us with the infinite.

Our higher journey is rooted in daily life transformations from waking to sleep. It does not exclude the world of the waking state but looks at it as just one phase of a much larger existence. It takes us beyond the dream of physical reality to the immutable reality of pure awareness.

As this inner movement of consciousness progresses, we learn to view the world as a symbol, intimation or imagination – not as real in itself but as the reflection of a mysterious internal reality beyond the senses and mind. We learn to view ourselves as spiritual aspirants on a life pilgrimage, following an eternal mission to unfold a higher awareness, not merely as a human person who derives from or belongs to this material world. This reality of the higher Self is what the profound traditions of Yoga and Vedic knowledge teach us. Our true nature is pure consciousness that underlies but also transcends all that we can see or do.

Today the human species stands at a very crucial stage in its evolution and in the unfoldment of its intelligence. Over the past few centuries, humanity has made enormous gains in scientific knowledge and technological expertise. Yet the basic egoistic urges of desire, greed and the seeking for power and domination remain intact even in our leaders. We remain trapped in an external view of reality, perhaps more so than our less technological ancestors. The new technology has not yet brought us a higher inner vision, but is adding greater confusion. We use these extraordinary new inventions to get more enmeshed in the outer world, not to free ourselves from its compulsions.

We make these powerful new machines into more destructive weapons, not just tools for better living. Information technology not only provides more detailed ways of looking at the external world; it can also stifle intuition and reduce our ability to perceive the subtle nuances of the diverse cosmos. Sophisticated communication devices can inhibit or substitute for real human relationships, and leave us inwardly isolated. We are becoming mechanical ourselves, losing connections both with the world of nature around us and our true inner nature, whose existence we have little recognition of.

Today we need not merely a new technology but also a new human being to operate the technology properly with wisdom and compassion – one whose intelligence is not dependent upon the machine and whose identity is not dependent upon the media, but who can think creatively beyond the need for any external stimulation.

Changing consciousness in a fundamental manner has become a necessity today for the very survival of our species. We must move from an outer view of the world as matter, energy or information to an inner view of the world as a manifestation of a universal consciousness. Our current civilizational mentality has not developed sufficiently to properly manage this powerful new technology or to prevent it from becoming a more dangerous tool for war or commercial exploitation.

Yet what does such a real change of consciousness consist of? It is not just another change of mind as our thoughts are always changing anyway. Most of us change our minds regularly but that does not fundamentally alter who we are or how we perceive the world. A true change of consciousness requires a transformation from a fixation on the outer world of name and form to an inner Self-awareness that does not rely upon any external reference to define itself.

Such a change of consciousness is extremely difficult to achieve, particularly given the degree of social conditioning and the outward focus of our education and work activity. Yet if even a few individuals can accomplish this great task, it can change the world in a remarkable manner and bring in a new flow of grace and harmony for all.

Modern science offers many new methods to alter our brains and minds, through new developments in technology, the media and pharmacology. Yet these factors remain on the outside as the product of an outer view of the human being as only physical. They cannot substantially change our underlying consciousness, our understanding of who we are, or the reality in which we live. This can only be accomplished from the inside.

Science is now developing artificial intelligence (AI), not just to make life more convenient but even to tell us what to do – as if letting ourselves be ruled by robots and computers constitutes humanity's future evolution and a better way of life and higher intelligence for coming generations. We are trapped in an ever more complex material world and complicated outer view of ourselves, extending to media images and virtual reality. We have forgotten our inner being – our capacity to rest content in who we are and a living relationship with the universe of nature.

Going Beyond Materialism and Physical Reality

For all the apparent advancement in civilization, we continue to define life in terms of physical reality aiming at personal enjoyment through the senses, much like previous generations. We strive to improve our lives through physical manipulations and acquisitions, including property, wealth, power and social recognition. We remain largely the same old creatures but with a quickly changing technology that provides the illusion that we are really changing ourselves. This is like trying to improve our lives by changing the clothes that we wear, not by awakening to our inner being beyond all appearances.

Our current civilization, which is largely a product of the western world, has developed the material sciences for exploiting the external world and its hidden energies from electricity to nuclear power. But we have not yet adequately developed a corresponding inner science of consciousness that can truly transform our awareness from something limited and biased to the universal and cosmic.

Yet such an inner science of consciousness has existed in humanity for thousands of years – and has flourished more in the past, at least in certain parts of the world. It is better developed in ancient and eastern cultures, particularly those of the Himalayan region, India and Tibet, with their profound traditions of Yoga, meditation and mantra that are now gaining a worldwide influence and respect.

This Yoga tradition, which was started by the ancient Vedic

Rishis thousands of years ago, sustains an inner science of Self-realization. Numerous yogis and sages throughout the ages have developed an inner knowledge of consciousness, connecting the human mind with the Cosmic Mind and with the Supreme Consciousness beyond all time and space.

This inner consciousness tradition remains alive and its wisdom continues to be accessible with global communication, if we approach it with sincerity, humility and introspection. Yet at the same time the modern commercialization of Yoga presents a diminished version of the tradition, keeping people trapped in body and mind, rather than developing a consciousness beyond these. This deeper Yoga tradition rests upon a profound individual search and is not a matter of the marketplace today.

Exploration of Consciousness

I have been working with Vedic teachings on various levels for several decades, from Yoga and Vedanta, to Ayurveda and Vedic astrology. I have become convinced of their profound relevance and efficacy, and the need to share their insights as best possible. These consciousness-based teachings show us how to connect to the cosmic reality within oneself beyond all beliefs, concepts and imaginations. They bring us a different type of knowledge that cannot be limited by words and concepts but is a matter of direct cognition much more vivid than what the senses allow us to perceive.

My long-term meditation practice drew me into a silent meditative state before sleep, shutting off the mind, letting go of all the complications of the day, moving from outer transient concerns to an inner exploration of timeless awareness. This enabled me to enter into sleep with a mind detached and turned within, allowing me to continue a meditative state throughout the night. I would awaken early in the morning, the time of Brahma Muhurta around 4 AM, and expand that meditative state further, at which time I could more easily experience the vibrations of the Cosmic Mind and a universal sense of Being.

Over time this meditative exploration came to permeate my sleep state, with a pattern of inner wakefulness continuing throughout the night, even when the body was fast asleep. Ordinary sleep disappeared and became a contemplative state, in which my mind could examine the key issues of who we are and the nature of reality, detaching from body and mind, and gradually merging into an awareness without division.

I began to experience an inner awakening in the dream state. Sometimes I would stop the dream and move into a deeper formless realm of awareness. Other times I would play with the dream and expand the power of imagination, as in an artistic inspiration, or vision quest. I could eventually contact dream worlds and subtle experiences with a deep inspiration, connected to other lives and other dimensions of existence beyond the physical and the human.

Eventually this continued awareness continued into the state of deep sleep, with the imaginative mind of the dream state put to rest. This brought in deeper experiences and realizations, a mergence into a formless reality of light, energy, vibration, awareness, peace and bliss, extending into the infinite and eternal, into realms of meditation not defined by name or form.

This inner awareness then came to linger during the day, when I could, as it were, shut the mind off, and enter into a thought free awareness – or I could let the mind continue but move my consciousness into a state of observation in which the mind was only a tool, not my true nature. I learned to turn the mind off at will and dwell in that formless state as needed. Or I could function in the outer world with my inner consciousness awake, using the outer mind to deal with external affairs without being taken in by them.

Recognition of the Transcendent Self

One uses the term I here in a provisional sense, as this inner consciousness underlying waking, dream and deep sleep is not the waking ego or human mind, the ordinary self, but a deeper cosmic awareness ultimately beyond all ideas and concepts, which are but transient mental energies. I began to realize that my self or person in the waking state, in fact all people in the waking world, are but illusions or reflections of a deeper unitary consciousness. I came to experience the waking state as an extended or collective dream – a web of appearances that must be carefully examined to discover the underlying reality that can be very different than what the senses present us.

Our true Self, inner being and real person abides beyond all externality and has broad connections throughout all time and space to the transcendent and unmanifest. This Self exists within and behind both body and mind, which are external to it and only outer objects for its deeper vision.

The true Self or real person is neither body, nor mind, which are but instruments of action and expression for the karma of this particular birth. This inner consciousness dwells behind the senses, prana, mind and intellect as their witness, observer and operator.

Our primary ignorance in life is that we confuse our inner awareness with the outer instruments of body and mind, and through them get caught in the external world that they connect us to. In the process we lose our true Self, dignity and authenticity, which is self-sufficient. Instead we try to become someone or something in the external world as if we had no inner value of our own. We are driven by shifting desires and the need to accumulate things outwardly, as if we were only material things ourselves.

Our daily states of consciousness as waking, dream and deep sleep are but three operations of the mind as an instrument of perception. You are the inner person, the real being operating the mind, who transcends these three phases. As a center of pure consciousness, you can move beyond these outer states of mind into inner dimensions of awareness beyond the external world, or any individualized identity, into the Self-aware universe that is the manifestation of unlimited Being-Consciousness-Bliss.

The Eternal Teachings

The profound ancient *Upanishads* of India teach the path of Self-inquiry and the exploration of consciousness and are the fountainhead of this inner wisdom. These wisdom texts have long been my primary subject of study and contemplation for their wonderful dialogues and profound questions. The *Upanishads* have been the most important book in the formation of my thoughts and deeper experiences. Contemplating their teachings is not just an intellectual experience, but awakening an altogether different type of intelligence that does not depend upon words or concepts for understanding to take place.

The *Upanishads* consist of various teachings or ways of knowledge, called *vidyas*. Of these one of the most important is the knowledge of our daily three states of consciousness – waking, dream and deep sleep – and the fourth transcendent pure consciousness beyond (Turiya). This way of higher knowledge over time became a natural part of my meditative quest. I did not originally seek to follow this teaching by any specific intention. Rather it unfolded spontaneously in the course of my practice according to an inner impetus and secret guidance.

Many of us are looking for something Divine, transcendent or cosmic as the ultimate goal of life, for which we are willing to search beyond the ordinary world for something unknown and unbounded. Yet we fail to recognize that a divine and transcendent consciousness exists already at the very ground of our being. This unlimited awareness is latent behind the veil of deep sleep, out of which arises the limited knowledge and outer awareness that prevails in waking and dream states.

We only need to turn within and shut the mind off, and we will naturally move into the infinite. That inner switch, as it were, through which the mind can be silenced, can be discovered if we look deeply into the core awareness within our own hearts. This very willingness to transcend will take us beyond all outer limitations. You can discover your true Self and real Person as a deeper light and energy of consciousness at the core of your being, yet pervading all that you see from every side. This search for the inner Self is the focus of the exploration of consciousness that we will examine in this book.

The Yoga of Consciousness: the Supreme Yoga

Traditional Yoga, as defined in key Yoga texts like the *Yoga Sutras* and the *Bhagavad Gita,* is first of all a "Yoga of Consciousness", requiring a deepening and expansion of an inner awareness. It is not a mere Yoga of outer action or bodily movements, but a Yoga of meditative inquiry. Its primary approach is to develop a direct change of consciousness within us, not simply to adjust the body, senses or mind externally. The ancient Yoga teaches us to use the inner to change the inner, and does not depend upon external factors to change our awareness. Even the external factors it may employ consist of various methods of internalizing and slowing down our senses, prana and mind.

Such a lasting change of consciousness rests upon fundamental changes in attitudes, perceptions and values. It requires setting aside our old views of the personal self and old beliefs in the reality of the external world of the senses. This inner Yoga proceeds through deconditioning the mind and deconstructing physical reality, so that we can understand the all-pervasive light of awareness as the true nature of all existence. Yet compared to the outer yoga, the inner Yoga offers much more to our deeper heart and awareness, and can lead us to the highest truth, peace and happiness.

The *Yoga Sutras* defines Yoga as the control of the mind (chitta),[1] using the term mind here in the broadest sense as individualized consciousness, and not merely the intellect; extending from instinct to emotion, thought and intuition. This yogic mastery of the mind and its functions takes us to Self-realization, a return to the natural state of awareness of the true Self, the Purusha or Atman. Purusha or Atman is unbounded Self-existent consciousness, not any embodied creature or individualized mind.

Yoga is commonly defined as the union of the individual Self (Jivatman) with the transcendent Self (Paramatman), which is essentially a mergence into unlimited consciousness. The meditative movement of Yoga proceeds through the state of Samadhi or unitary awareness that is the highest of the eight limbs of Yoga practice.

The main practice of this inner Yoga consists of cultivating *moment-by-moment awareness*, without which our consciousness cannot fundamentally transform. This requires sustaining a steady awareness through every moment of change in body, mind and world. It requires calming the mind at a fundamental level and abiding in the inner state of the Seer.

Such a process of continuous awareness cannot be limited to a technique, posture, idea or action, which are secondary aids or preparatory practices. It is an on-going practice that has no beginning or end, as we find in the Yoga Sutra concept of abhyasa.[2] Dwelling in this moment-by-moment awareness, we can continue to function in the outer world as necessary, but our action will be rooted in an inner knowing, not in the mechanical, compulsive and habitual behavioral patterns of the mind.

Consciousness is Yoga

Consciousness itself is inherently a practice of Yoga. Whatever we do out of consciousness has a natural unifying, integrating or yogic effect. Consciousness itself is the ultimate balancing, energizing and renewing factor in all existence.

Yoga can be defined as the inherent action of consciousness to harmonize, attune and bring peace and unity to all that we do. Yoga requires continuous abiding awareness in thought and action. Yet this requires that we dwell in pure consciousness itself as the ultimate transformative power.

The Yoga of consciousness is the primary practice of Yoga. It is the supreme Yoga underlying all yogic paths and approaches, be it Hatha Yoga, Raja Yoga, or the Yogas of knowledge, devotion, service and ritual. True Yoga practice is based on developing unity consciousness.

Without an inner awareness, there is no real Yoga practice, whatever we may try to do. An unconscious or half-aware Yoga is not Yoga at all – it does not bring about inner awakening but only a continued sleep in the outer world. Yoga properly understood is the means to realize the highest consciousness within us as our true nature. Whatever we do as a Yoga practice should be performed with care, discipline and a higher non-ego based motivation, rooted in an inner awareness.

There are many practices and methods that can be included in this greater Yoga of Consciousness as aids, support measures or preliminary procedures. All Yoga practices are originally meant to bring consciousness into the different aspects of our life and being, including how we move the body, how we breathe, how we use the senses and the mind, and how we function in the external world, both individually and with others. Yet consciousness is the prime factor of Yoga, not these outer aspects that we must integrate into an inner awareness for Yoga to truly unfold.

The most important Yoga practice that we must understand is the daily movement of our own consciousness. To master this we must hold to a continual awareness of the fluctuating states of the mind throughout the day. Of these shifting mental states, most dominant are the radical changes through waking, dream and deep sleep. The Yoga of consciousness as moment-by-moment awareness reaches its maturity when we can maintain continuous awareness through waking, dream and deep sleep, without any break, hiatus or diminution.

This inner Yoga requires controlling our minds to the extent that we can use the mind at will and turn off the mind's different functions of memory, emotion, thought or sensation, if we need to. Actually the mind is constantly going off and on, firing like a series of rapid lightning flashes if we look deeply at its shifting movements. To turn the mind off, we begin by extending the space of our awareness and the gap between our thoughts, eventually moving beyond thought to the space of pure observation. Our thought patterns are but surface waves on a deeper ocean of consciousness that we can merge into once we know how to turn within.

Meaning of Consciousness

Consciousness is a term that has a range of meanings in the English language and yet other implications in Yoga and Vedanta, which have several specific terms for Consciousness and its different functions. Consciousness in modern usage can refer to any type of awareness, individual or collective. There is some form of consciousness in everything, however rudimentary it may be. This rudimentary consciousness can be described as some sense of existence or intelligent patterning to action or energy.

Consciousness in a rudimentary form is hidden in inanimate matter down to the level of subatomic particles that follow mathematical laws in their movement. Most of us doubt whether the stars, planets, and galaxies are in some sense Self-aware. Looking contemplatively at the night sky, one intuits that this must be so. There is a grandeur to the cosmos that appears as a manifestation of a deep intelligence, not a random evolution of unconscious forces.

Consciousness progressively manifests itself in the evolution of life; asleep but developing in minerals with their geometrical patterns of growth, slowly awakening in the plants with the movement of their sap, their seasons, growth and flowering, and expressing itself through the instrumentality of the mind and senses starting with animals, which gain a power of independent movement.

Human beings represent a further evolution of consciousness, developing a sense of individual identity – including a recognition of values, truth and falsehood, right and wrong, good and evil. On top of this, we have a special capacity to cultivate consciousness directly through meditation, taking us potentially beyond creaturely mind to universal awareness. Very few of us can do this as a primary activity in life, and not all cultures make meditation into an integral part of life, but it is a potential that we all possess and can develop further.

We can discriminate three general levels of consciousness, which cross over to some degree.

- The first is consciousness as a general principle in nature, which all the forces of nature hold to some degree, and through which the laws of nature function. This consciousness permeates nature from the most minute to the most vast levels, extending to the very cosmic intelligence responsible for nature itself.

- The second is embodied or individualized consciousness, which is the mind of living creatures, starting from the mineral to the plant, animal, human and beyond. This is what most of us of us know as consciousness.

- The third is consciousness as a universal principle behind and beyond the universe and all creatures within it - the pure consciousness of unlimited Self-awareness. This is the goal of all true spiritual aspiration.

In Yogic thought, this higher or transcendent consciousness is called *Chit,* while embodied consciousness is called *chitta,* which is the mind in creatures. Chit is part of a trinity of cosmic principles as Sat-Chit-Ananda or Being-Consciousness-Bliss absolute, which are the three aspects of unitary existence. In this regard, rudimentary and even mental states of consciousness are not Consciousness in its true reality but mere reflections of it bound by error and illusion. Until we dwell in pure Consciousness we cannot get beyond ignorance and wrong judgment.

Consciousness and Mindfulness

The yogic view of consciousness is of a higher awareness that transcends the human mind, which is a limited intelligence bound by creaturely and social imperatives. Mindfulness, similarly, implies being aware of the mind, observing our thoughts, emotions and sensations rather than simply getting caught in their reactions. Yogic mindfulness implies being aware of the mind from the standpoint of the witnessing consciousness, the Atman or Purusha, the seer as mentioned in the *Yoga Sutras.*

Exploring the Yoga of Consciousness

We will explore this deeper Yoga of Consciousness through the Yoga of the Four States of Waking, Dream, Deep Sleep and Turiya or the Transcendent Fourth. We will also bring in other aspects of this Yoga of Consciousness and its relationship to the Yoga tradition as a whole. All of Yoga rests upon our daily states of mind and the inner consciousness underlying them.

Every Yoga practice gains greater meaning according to how we connect it to an inner awareness.

A true Yogi is one who has merged into the inner being of pure consciousness beyond body and mind. He or she uses the body and mind as instruments of a higher awareness, not for purposes of personal enjoyment. Such true yogis do not believe in physical reality or mental formulas. They are not identified with their bodies, senses, mind, social appearances or recognition in the outer world. They do not need anything material to make them happy. They are not seeking anything from other people. They are not trying to impose any ideas, beliefs or needs upon others. Their sole goal is sharing the freedom and self-sufficiency of consciousness that is one with all.

May we all become such true Yogis! Then whatever we do will be of an enduring benefit for all. For this we must follow the inherent Yoga of Consciousness in the spiritual pilgrimage and yogic journey that is the essence of our short sojourn on this Earth. Let us open our inner eye and inner heart to move along this path!

Self-awareness: the Ultimate Reality

There is only one ultimate reality – an all-pervading Self-awareness beyond time, space and causation. All manifestations of matter, energy, life and mind are but appearances or aspects of this deeper consciousness in different dimensions and expressions, with no reality apart from it.

The universe as a whole is Self-aware – a single conscious being with various diversifications, like the limbs and organs of our own bodies, extending from the infinitesimal into the Infinite. We possess an intuition of such a deeper Self and immorality within us that provides us a soul memory of a cosmic reality far exceeding our transient human lives.

This background Self-awareness transcends the manifest universe, which consists of waves and vibrations at the surface of its boundless Being. It holds all the time/space and form-based worlds as its outer dimension, with a greater timeless, non-localized reality as its true essence. Discovering and living in this supreme Self-awareness is our highest purpose and wellbeing that we must make central in all that we do.

Self-Awareness in the Human Being

As individual human beings, each one of us can be defined first of all by self-awareness. Our degree of human self-consciousness and reflective thinking distinguishes us from the animal kingdom. We are not only capable of action, we can reflect upon what we have done and observe its consequences for good or ill. We recognize the human being as an independent intelligence responsible for who it is and what it does. We can create enduring values of truth and falsehood, right and wrong that extend beyond any changing personal and biological needs.

If we examine our mental activity carefully, we will observe that we are first of all aware of ourselves and then only later become aware of other objects or what could be called the not-self. *Our self-awareness is direct, existential, foundational and continuous, whereas our awareness of external factors is indirect, phenomenal (perceptible by the senses), superficial and transient.*

The sense of self within us remains the same while the objects and energies that it contacts on the outside are ever changing. Without some continuity to our sense of self, we would have no continuity, unity or coherence for body or mind or anything else that we experience. Self-awareness is the very ground of our existence, not the external world that we perceive indirectly through the senses.

Yet we do not ordinarily experience this pure Self-awareness in its true nature. Our minds are fixated externally through the senses and we seldom look within. We are continually distracted from seeing our true nature. Though the ground of being is within us, we are entranced in the play of becoming outside of ourselves, including many things and events that do not really concern us at all. We are like a person who fails to look at who he or she actually is but instead is caught up in their possessions, clothing or equipment as most important, or the gossip and worry about other people.

We are normally aware of ourselves only in relation to other creatures and objects on the outside. We are immersed in a "relational self" or "I-project" and seldom experience a direct Self-awareness without any external object, except in the state of deep sleep, which we forget every day. Ignoring our Self-nature we project a self-idea outside of ourselves, our self-image as a person in the external world, which we pretend is who we truly are.

This "relational" or "referred self" is not a pure Self-awareness, but consists of an internalization of how we regard that others see us. Our sense of self is based upon how we project ourselves relative to an assumed reality of other people, letting society define us and seeking recognition and identity through it. We get caught in our self-image and miss the imageless light of our true nature without which nothing could be known. We confuse our internal consciousness with objective factors starting with our own bodies – which is to lose our eternal Self-identity for transient outer identifications.

The result is that we do not know who in essence we truly are. Our identity remains in question and compromised, a changing construct of shifting factors relative to the transient world around us – a kaleidoscope, cavalcade and panorama of thoughts, emotions, sensations and external connections. Instead of being who we truly are, we search for recognition in the world of the not-self, trying to be someone that we are not that others will recognize, honor and reward.

This dilemma of our identity is compounded by the shadow of what we were in the past, and the imagination, speculation or dream of who we might be in the future. Instead of being what we are in the present, we are in search of an imagined self through the movement of time. The result is that our lives are caught in illusion, if not confusion, with only fleeting moments of clarity, peace and happiness. We are busy chasing or projecting appearances, forgetting our intrinsic nature, which is witness of all. And sadly we become so blinded by the outer world that we believe in an outer ego identity and forget our deeper unity consciousness.

Moving from Limited to Unlimited Self-awareness

Besides the "unlimited Self-awareness" of the greater universe, which is the higher reality at a cosmic level, there is the "limited self-awareness" of the embodied creature, consisting of who we are in our creaturely lives. There are only these two primary factors in the universe, we could say, as unlimited or as limited Self-awareness, though the two are related. Limited self-awareness rests upon and manifests from unlimited Self-awareness. Limited self-awareness is the individualized ego, while unlimited Self-awareness is universal consciousness.

Limited self-awareness is the mind and embodied soul shadowed by ignorance. It consists of self-awareness experienced through the limiting filters of the mind, senses and physical body. Our primary error of perception is that we confuse an intrinsic Self-awareness with a limited ego identity, the true Self with body and mind. This is like confusing the moon with a lake in which it is reflected. We seek unlimited truth, happiness and existence in limited forms and actions that are changing every moment, leaving us in eventual sorrow.

Yoga in its original sense is a path of meditative inquiry moving from limited self-awareness to unlimited Self-awareness – from the limited "I am the body" identity to the unlimited "I am all" that embraces the entire universe. Yoga is the path of Self-awareness, returning our embodied self-awareness with the unlimited Self-awareness responsible for all existence. This is the union that Yoga is based upon, a mergence into unitary consciousness.

Our lives consist of an ongoing movement in awareness, through various thoughts, feelings, sensations and states of consciousness day-by-day and moment-by-moment. This movement of awareness is largely subliminal rather than conscious, a movement in limited awareness, struggling to expand, yet bound by inertia, unconsciousness, sleep and dream. We are striving to be aware, but succeed only partially and temporarily.

We are constantly trying to learn more about life during wakeful hours, yet we find that life overflows us on every side, with our minds only capable of grasping a few pinpoint fragments of the vast stream of events. While we can become informed, erudite or experts on various topics, eventually we must die and pass into the great unknown, continuing a greater spiritual journey that we do not comprehend in our ordinary lives. Ours is a limited awareness seeking to expand its boundaries recognizing that an unlimited awareness is possible.

To know our true identity, we must first understand our deeper Self-identity. The best way to do this is to cultivate a moment-by-moment awareness. A pure Self-awareness is present at both the center and the periphery of all of our thoughts. By learning to remain conscious of that inner center, rather than external objects, we can gradually unfold all the secrets of our own lives and of the greater cosmic life as well.

True awareness is always self-awareness and is not circumscribed by any limits of name and form that are its perceptions. Whatever we experience, however apparently external, remains part of our own consciousness like the waves of the sea. Cultivating Self-awareness is the essence of life and the practice of Yoga. It includes all things but does not give them any separate reality.

Self-awareness is the foundation of the exploration of our states of consciousness that the following chapters will examine in depth. *It requires living in consciousness rather than simply appearing in the outer world, holding to awareness as reality rather than material things*. We must learn to give up our desires for external objects for a deeper aspiration to know the inner truth. This will eventually allow us to discover the entire universe within us.

Our lives are a quest for higher awareness, a search within for a deeper reality of both Self and universe that unites the two. We should not let our lives be defined by mere physical, commercial or intellectual factors. We should not limit ourselves to the body and mind, but should open up and surrender to the Divine within, which is our true Self that pervades all space. Instead of being bound to a self-image, we will discover that the entire universe is but a reflection of our own inner awareness.

Modern Science and the Science of Consciousness

India's civilization over thousands of years has made the inner science of consciousness its primary concern, more so than religion as faith or the development of the material sciences. The great minds of Indian or Bharatiya culture have pursued the path of meditation to discover the core of awareness within us as their most important endeavor. Dharmic civilization, such as centered in India, recognizes that the inquiry into the nature of consciousness is the most important pursuit for all human beings, whether in one's personal life or in the collective search for truth.

Outer sciences like medicine, physics, astronomy and biology certainly have their place in making our lives safer and more productive and helping us to better utilize the natural forces around us. Yet these outer sciences remain secondary because, however much they help us externally, they cannot provide lasting answers to the ultimate questions of who we are, the nature of reality, and what if anything within us transcends death. *They do not fundamentally change our consciousness but only provide more information and better outer functioning.*

The inner science of consciousness is the supreme science because only through it can we truly understand the nature of the universe, its origin and goal – and the nature of our inner being that is not limited to body and mind. The highest knowledge is Self-knowledge, knowing who we are in the essence of our being. Without this inner knowing we get caught in the errors and illusions of the mind and in a fixation on transient phenomena as reality. Only the science of meditation provides us with the direct experience of the Infinite and Eternal. It cannot be brought about by any technology, outer experiments or group actions.

New Views of Science

Modern science with its many new research projects is slowly developing a new view of consciousness better aligned with dharmic traditions as compared to the old fixed material view of the world of pre-relativity science. That the world of the senses is an illusion is now a scientific fact, though science is not certain as to what the ultimate reality or truth behind it may be. Science is making progress towards recognizing the transcendence of Consciousness, though it may not yet have reached its decisive turn towards inner knowing.

Science is approaching consciousness in two primary ways.

- The first is through quantum physics that is proposing a unitary field of consciousness underlying the universe to explain the coherence of the laws of nature. So far this universal field of consciousness is but a theory and not all scientists accept it. Scientists are looking for a way to measure it, but have no defined system for understanding its possible reality inside us.

  This universal field of consciousness is well known to Vedic thought as Brahman, Being-Consciousness-Bliss Absolute. It constitutes the Vedic view of God, the Divine or the supreme reality, the origin and end of all. Yet Vedic thought recognizes other universals like a cosmic intelligence as the repository of the laws of nature, and a universal prana or all-pervasive life-force. Under its Purusha theory, Yoga regards the universe as a single organic being, a cosmic human being.

- The second level of the scientific approach to consciousness is through modern neuroscience, which includes mapping the brain, its functions and energies.

  This new study of the brain is discovering the healing powers of Yoga and meditation for mental health and proper neurological functioning. Yet so far it has not understood the subtle energy and mind fields beyond the physical body that meditation masters are also able to explore. It examines mind function through brain chemistry or media manipulations. Its main treatment for the mind consists of new pharmaceutical drugs that are powerful but dangerous, complicating how we live and think. A yogic neuroscience links the brain to deeper powers of consciousness beyond the body and external world. It does not require any drugs or technology for its applications.

Both these scientific approaches remain outward in orientation with only an intimation of the inner, not recognizing the primacy of consciousness over anything external, including the scientific mind and its discourse. Modern science remains far from embracing consciousness as the supreme reality, though its own logic may inevitably lead it there.

Physics looks at consciousness through the mathematics of physical forces that are but its shadows. Neuroscience identifies the brain as the origin of mind and consciousness, a view that limits consciousness to the body and physical reality. It makes chemical medicine the main method for treating mental dysfunctions, as if these were merely dysfunctions of a mechanical nature, instead of consequences of an independent intelligence and its actions. Until Consciousness is given its inherent value, such scientific approaches will remain limited, though they cannot ultimately deny the awareness that permeates all existence.

Brain, Mind and Consciousness

Vedic thought teaches that the brain, mind, and consciousness are fundamentally different in nature, though related in function. The physical brain is but an instrument for the mind, but the mind also has its own level of existence extending beyond physical reality. The core mind, consisting of our karmic patterns, leaves the body at death and eventually moves on to another body for another physical life – a fact which many yogis, mystics and occultists are aware of.

Yet the mind, which has its own structure and function, is not the origin of consciousness either. The mind is but an instrument for a deeper consciousness, orienting it to time, space and practical reality. Mind is a composite consciousness of conditioned responses, memories and capacities, not a self-aware intelligence. It has its subtle material nature and is part of the external world.

The true Self dwells beyond body and mind and is the real source of awareness, not limited by change, action, name or form. This *Atman* or inner Self is one with *Brahman* or the universal consciousness, as Vedic thought proposes. Universal consciousness and embodied consciousness or mind are linked, but cannot be made identical. We must surrender our minds to the consciousness within by making them silent, receptive and calm like a mirror.

Operating the physical brain and its chemistry is what could be called the "subtle brain of energy and awareness", the thousand-petal lotus, the highest of the seven *chakras* of yogic thought. This lotus of the head allows us to manifest the secrets of higher consciousness, but must be first awakened by yogic practices of pranayama, mantra and meditation to truly come into function. It is largely dormant or unevolved in the ordinary person and not easily developed without special yogic efforts that may extend over several lifetimes.

When modern science explores the brain in order to understand consciousness, it is like measuring a person by examining the movements of their shadow. Vedic thought teaches us first how to transcend the brain along with its biological limitations and compulsions; and second how to transcend the mind, which is individualized consciousness, to move beyond conditioned karmic limitations. This leads us to pure Consciousness, which is an all-pervasive universal principle like space. It requires going to the core of our awareness that persists through waking, dream and deep sleep. It also raises the possibility that in sleep and in other states of awareness, we can access higher aspects of reality than the physical, which is but one level of consciousness, not the whole or the essence of it.

If there is a unitary field of consciousness underlying the universe, it must be accessible to the human mind, as it exists everywhere. By linking our human mind with this cosmic intelligence, we can transcend the limitations and biases of our species. But this requires recognizing our immortal nature beyond its current embodiment. It means going beyond human conditioning, language and sensory perception.

Science and the Four States of Consciousness

Science today remains a science of the waking state, focused on the physical body, brain and material world. To understand our true Self we need a science of all four states of consciousness: waking, dream, deep sleep and the cosmic fourth state beyond. This is the yogic science of consciousness. No merely physical or bodily-based science can uncover the deeper secrets of universal consciousness that is beyond all manifestations of matter, energy and mind. It requires an inner vision and aspiration, an inward turning of life, mind and behavior.

We must move beyond the science of the waking state to a science of all the four states. The true scientist or inquirer into reality is not the self of the waking state, but is the Self that underlies all the four states and is beyond body and mind. The scientist of the waking state is a dream and his or her knowledge of the waking world is ultimately dream knowledge, not direct knowledge of reality.

Modern science is still very much a product of a spiritual ignorance, though it is evolving towards a higher knowledge. It has developed from an outer sense-based knowledge, not from a certain inner intuition. For a real science of consciousness to emerge we must move beyond the ignorance of the mind to the light of universal awareness. We must look beyond the external known or unknown to the inner knower and seer.

The great yogis of India teach a practical way to bring about this radical change in awareness, but it involves extensive changes in our values, perception and activity, not just outer experimentations or intellectual analysis. Scientists today are still asleep in the dream of physical reality, but are beginning to wake up as we discover that the physical world is as much a reflection of how the brain works, as it is an objective reality. The brain itself is another level of the same illusory set of appearances. The more we examine outer appearances, from solid matter to the subtle energies causing it, the more these disappear into an underlying space that is Self-aware and complete within itself.

Looking Beyond Science to Direct Knowing

In this book, we will not examine in detail how modern science views waking, dream and deep sleep from biological, physiological or brain-based perspectives. These have their validity at an outer level but are not valid or final at an inner level. They are judgments and views of the waking state and physical body. Our inquiry is into the Self that underlies all the four states, for whom the waking state is but a secondary manifestation.

We need to examine deeper questions beyond physical or quantitative reality. These include who we are in our true nature, why we are alive, and how the consciousness within us transcends body and mind. In this regard scientific knowledge of brain function is of secondary value. What is more important is our own meditative self-experience and a deeper level of consciousness beyond any attachment to physical or mental reality. So let us look beyond the outer intellect and awaken an inner intelligence that transcends all theories, numbers, and constructs. Let us learn to live, see and breathe within our own awareness, consciousness-to-consciousness, ever present and beyond time and death.

Part II

The Yoga of the Four States of Consciousness

The Yoga of the Four States of Consciousness

Many secrets of deeper Yoga practices exist that are unknown today. Only a few of these have been divulged in the available Yoga literature and seldom completely. What may be called deeper yogic teachings are mere formulas or techniques, generally simplified, which without the proper background and adaptation cannot take us beyond our ordinary state of mind.

Most of what is today called *Yoga Nidra*, with various yogic approaches to sleep and relaxation, remains preliminary. There are many deeper teachings of yogic states of samadhi, mergence, absorption and transcendence, which connect to important meditation practices of Yoga and Vedanta. We must remember that yogic teachings reflect a very different view of the universe and of humanity than our current civilization, making Consciousness the ultimate goal and reality, not our mere physical existence.

Today Yoga teachings, whose real aim is a radical change of consciousness, are used to enhance physical and mental well-being rather than to reach a higher level of awareness. Like the labor required to produce a great work of art, true Yoga requires tremendous concentration, focus and determination. It rests upon an inner inspiration and a flow of grace from a higher Divine light. It is an individual practice that varies according to each person and the movement of their karma.

Yet great Yoga secrets can be discovered as part of our daily lives, hidden underneath our natural rhythms and actions. Secrets of higher awareness are latent in how we see, think, speak and breathe – and in the movements of lives throughout the days, months, seasons and years. The shifting levels of awareness from waking to sleep hold important transformative powers that we seldom appreciate.

Of these ancient yogic secrets very important is the "Yoga of the Four States of Consciousness". This refers to the three states of waking, dream and deep sleep, along with the fourth state of ever-wakeful, peaceful and blissful consciousness known as Turiya, the state of Self-awareness beyond the body and mind.

The Yoga of the Four States is not simply an asana, pranayama nor mantra practice. It is not based upon a particular formula or technique that can be performed by a group of people together. It does not follow any specific schedule of classes or routines. It can employ a number of methods under certain conditions but is not defined by any one of these, as they are but provisional aids.

The Yoga of the Four States is the essence of the greater Yoga of Consciousness that consists of sustaining a moment-by-moment awareness throughout the day, including during sleeping hours. It is characterized by a continued state of seeing, and not by the performance of any outer or inner action.

The Yoga of Consciousness moves from the internal to the external, bringing our outer life under the control of an inner awareness. This is different from the outer motivation of our lives, in which we try to change ourselves internally by doing something externally, be it changing our location in the outer world, moving our bodies differently, or bringing new ideas or information into the mind.

This Yoga of Consciousness is, simply speaking, the practice of being continually present, awake and aware as an inner state of being. Such an ongoing awareness does not mean to merely dwell in the present moment or pursue immediate sensations, but to abide in the presence of consciousness that transcends all time. It leads us to sustaining attention, concentration and meditation throughout the day.

The Yoga of Consciousness is an extension of the principle of *abhyasa* or practice of Yoga as defined in the *Yoga Sutras.* In this regard, the *Yoga Sutras* refers to gaining "knowledge of the support (*avalambana*) of dream and sleep" as one of the most important means of gaining steadiness of mind.[3] It requires reaching the foundation of our inner being behind the thoughts and actions of our outer lives.

All techniques, whether physical or mental, become mechanical if we do not sustain an awareness during their practice, as they easily draw us into a state of conditioned response and memorized behavior. *There is no mechanical method for keeping us inwardly awake*. Nothing from the external world can bring it about. There is no en masse practice to develop direct perception at an individual level. The true awakening of consciousness occurs only when we move beyond all formulas and compulsions and directly contact our inner nature.

There is no magic sequence of asanas that can fundamentally change our consciousness, however helpful these may be at physical or psychological levels. There is no fixed mantra, to be repeated a certain number of times, through which we will quickly arrive at a transformation of consciousness. There is no secret meditation technique that will automatically transport everyone who performs it into everlasting bliss.

There are many yogic practices that can aid in a radical change of awareness, if applied according to a deeper inspiration, but we must not get caught in any outer forms as sufficient. Such practices will vary person-by-person, day-by-day and moment-by-moment, like an ever-new discovery. Eventually they must mirror a continual state of awareness, in which all outer forms become peripheral. Every aspect of Yoga must be done in accord an inner consciousness, which is the real transforming factor. The goal of Yoga is to move beyond body and mind, not simply to develop them further.

The Practice of Continual Awareness

The Yoga of the Four States requires that we let go of all the dogmas, formulas and beliefs of the mind. It cannot be institutionalized or made into a set procedure for everyone. It requires cultivating our own continuous awareness or *svanubhava* in Sanskrit. As each moment is different, we must be ever ready for the new, the unexpected and unplanned.

The Yoga of the Four States is one of the main approaches of the direct path to Self-realization that forms the essence of *Jnana Yoga*, the "Yoga of Knowledge". Yet it is not the practice of a method but the practice of observation. One can move immediately into the fourth state at any moment we become receptive to the true Self within. Yet in whatever way we approach our inner Self and unity consciousness, it will naturally begin to pervade our waking, dream and deep sleep states, opening their veils and revealing the secret light behind them.

The Yoga of the Four States is best understood in Vedantic terms of Self-realization, knowing the true Self that is one with all. But it is not limited to any abstract philosophy or metaphysics as a mere intellectual pursuit. It is not a speculative theory or rational dialectic, much less a theology or ideology. It is rooted in the most basic factors of our lives, understanding the daily movements of our minds and developing detachment from them. This detachment from body and mind, person and world is the basis of true awareness that has no external referent or dependency.

Yet such an ongoing awareness is very far from the ordinary mind and its continual fluctuations. Throughout the day our mind's continuity of attention is broken by various distractions and periods of loss of attention altogether. We are constantly coming in and out of a state of attention, as the focus of our thoughts dissipates and varies in an unpredictable manner. Our mind's power of attention is limited both to the extent of the field that it covers and to the duration it can be sustained. We often lapse into phases of inattention or externalization of the mind, as in the pursuit of entertainment and sensation, losing our inner moorings altogether.

Our most notable lapse or discontinuity in awareness is our daily immersion in the state of sleep in which waking needs and compulsions are temporarily and happily forgotten. Yet this process of sleep unknown to us contains the potential to develop a higher awareness beyond mind and ego. The mystery of sleep contains the mystery of our deeper existence and that of the universe as a whole, the Brahman of Vedanta.

The Yoga of the Four States shows us how to develop a continuous awareness throughout the three lower states of waking, dream and deep sleep, so that we can reach an ever-wakeful state of transcendent awareness as the fourth state beyond them. Its practice enables us to turn the entire day and night, and all of its shifts of consciousness, into an ongoing and deepening meditation practice. We can use the natural movement of waking and sleep, as well as the special junctures between them, to access the universal consciousness that resides at the core of our being and to connect to the cosmic reality.

Yoga Nidra: Yogic Sleep and Mergence

Much of what is discussed in the Yoga of the Four States is examined in Yoga Nidra, which is becoming a popular and important part of Yoga practice today. There are many levels of Yoga Nidra, which is not only yogic sleep but yogic dissolution of the mind, extending from physical relaxation to complete transcendence of body and mind.

Yoga Nidra is one of the key aspects of traditional Yoga practice, particularly as part of deep meditation and inquiry approaches, such as are found in the Upanishads. Yet diverse forms of relaxation and pratyahara are now being taught under the umbrella of Yoga Nidra. Most of these are only preliminary practices to true Yoga Nidra, which involves merging into the deeper consciousness underlying sleep and dream. While outer Yoga Nidra is about relaxation of the body, inner Yoga Nidra is about going beyond the cosmic dream of time and space to the eternal and the infinite.

True Yoga Nidra cannot be done as part of a group class, scheduled session, or a preplanned program, however helpful these may be initially. True Yoga Nidra is not an activity of the individual person, the body or the mind. It is not merely a physical relaxation or a type of psychological stress relief. It requires putting the entire world and all levels of the mind to rest. It is the state of laya or mergence of all that is.

True Yoga Nidra is about tracing our consciousness from waking to dream, deep sleep and the transcendent Self. Relaxing the body is the first level only.

Such practices as pratyahara based relaxation aids in the process, but besides the pratyahara of the body there is also the pratyahara of the mind. This deeper pratyahara also consists of withdrawal from the mind, its conditioning and karmic patterns, including detachment from all mental activities. It is best done at an individual level as part of a deeper sadhana; and not as a kind of group practice, which might instead get us caught in the dream state or in the minds of other people that keep our imagination active.

True Yoga Nidra is an integral part of the Yoga of the Four States and is connected to cultivating wakefulness throughout all the three states of waking, dream, and deep sleep. It involves moving into the inner peace of the witness Self at the time of sleep or rest. It allows us to consciously enter into the state of deep sleep like a deep pratyahara; it also gives us the ability to shut off the sense and motor organs during the waking state as needed. In true Yoga Nidra, like deep sleep, we withdraw our consciousness into the deeper spiritual heart, which is the root and origin of ego, mind, prana and sensory activities.

When the mind is suspended in the state of Yoga Nidra, one can contact the free flow of wisdom from the higher conscious realm, its gurus and deity forms and higher lokas or realms of experience.[4] This is where higher Yoga teachings spontaneously arise and can be received. Through true Yoga Nidra we contact the consciousness of Ishvara, the inner teacher or Adi Guru of Yoga. Yoga Nidra takes us to dwelling in the Fourth State when the mind and senses are in withdrawal. It opens us to transcendent currents of knowledge and bliss. In this meditative Yoga Nidra we are asleep to the outer world but active in the realms of unbounded consciousness.

The Yoga of Deep Sleep is Yoga Nidra or yogic sleep in the deeper sense of the term, which is yogic mergence into unitary reality. True Yoga Nidra is entering consciously into the state of deep sleep and gradually merging deep sleep into the transcendent state of pure Self-awareness.

We will discuss this issue of Yoga Nidra further relative to the fourth state of Turiya, in the context of Vedantic meditation. The Yoga of Consciousness is also teaching Yoga Nidra but in a broader context of all the four states.

The Yoga of the Four States and Mantra

The Yoga of the Four States has a special connection with Mantra Yoga and primordial sound, Pranava, and with Nada Yoga and sound vibration, what is called Spanda in Sanskrit. This is not just a matter of repeating sounds or of chanting but of discovering the vibratory movement of the consciousness that operates all the movements in the universe and forms the core energy of our awareness.

Each of the four states has its particular vibratory rate that informs and sustains the level of consciousness within it. The movement from one of these four states of consciousness to another consists of a quantum shift in vibratory levels.

- The waking state has a vibratory connection to the external world of the senses and the pranic impulses that drive our outer activity, starting with waking speech and its patterns of expression, extending to biological and social compulsions.

- Dream closes off that waking vibration and opens up the vibration of our imagination that is only a shadow during waking hours. This dream vibration creates various dream sensations and experiences according to a much faster and internal vibratory rate than the waking state.

- Deep sleep closes the dream vibration off and merges us in an underlying tonality of latent awareness, like a background note with little vibratory change, but a subtle power of renewal.

As the Yoga Shakti or inner power of Yoga awakens, the inner sound current or OM vibration begins to resonate within us from the bottom of the spine to the top of the head and beyond in the cosmic space. The OM vibration is our natural connection with the fourth or highest state of awareness. The more we connect to OM, the more it will take us through all the four states in a single simultaneous vibration of sound and silence like a series of ascending waves. OM is the arrow, which is the single-minded focus that is the awakened Sushumna or central channel ascending into the infinite beyond the top of the head.

Mantra in its cosmic form as "vibratory resonance" is an important way to work with the four states of consciousness, through which we can naturally alter our field of awareness. Mantra Yoga is important in all Yoga approaches such as knowledge, devotion, service, action and prana. Mantra Yoga begins with chanting mantras out loud to bring their resonance into speech and mind, but is meant to eventually connect us to the vibratory state of Being, Consciousness and Bliss Absolute, Satchitananda, as deep silent meditative awareness.

The Kundalini Shakti, or inner power of Yoga, is identical with the arising of the OM vibration and has the power to carry our awareness to the fourth state. The chakras or energy centers of the subtle body open and unfold as we awaken to the vibratory power of pure consciousness underlying waking, dream and deep sleep. The fourth or transcendent state is both the expanse of the thousand petal lotus of the head and the core awareness in the spiritual heart. Our vibratory level crescendos from outer words and thoughts to Self-realization and the discovery of the entire universe, not just physical but subtle and causal, as contained within us, as we ourselves become a pure vibratory resonance of abiding awareness. While various practices help us do this, it is ultimately more of an inspiration that arises spontaneously within.

The Yoga of the Four States and Different Yoga Paths

The Yoga of the Four States is commonly referred to in traditional yogic teachings going back to the *Vedas*. It has a significant place in the classical *Upanishads* that form the fountainhead of Yoga and Vedanta.

- The Yoga of the Four States is a key practice of the Yoga of Knowledge (Jnana Yoga), which consists of the practice of Self-inquiry or an inner examination to discover our true nature beyond the mind and ego. This inner inquiry requires that we uncover the true Self behind waking, dream and deep sleep. It must be constant throughout the day and night in order to fully mature.

- The Yoga of the Four States is important in Raja or Ashtanga Yoga, as it teaches us how to control, neutralize and dissolve the mind in order to enter into a higher state of seeing. Deep sleep is our natural samadhi and shows us the way to silence the mind, if we can sustain an awareness through it. The natural state of the Seer or Purusha that the *Yoga Sutras* emphasize is that of the witness and the transcendent fourth state.

- The Yoga of the Four States has its place in Hatha Yoga, starting as related to practices of Pratyahara as sensory withdrawal and Yoga Nidra as yogic sleep expanding from that. Hatha Yoga uses various physical and mental techniques to aid in stilling the body, prana, senses and mind to reach the transcendent state.

  In this regard Hatha Yoga works from the outside to the inside, not from a direct change of consciousness as in Jnana Yoga, but in a clear and systematic manner that can help prepare the way.

  Pranayama helps us enter consciously into the deep sleep state, which is also state of pranic withdrawal or unitary prana. Pratyahara is a simulated deep sleep and Yoga Nidra is the yogic state of mergence as in the state of deep sleep, but with a sustained background focus and awareness.

- The Yoga of Devotion (Bhakti Yoga) has a subtle connection with the Yoga of the Four States. The spiritual heart that is the seat of the deity for devotional surrender is also the state of consciousness underlying deep sleep. Devotion or Bhakti is another important means to take us across waking and sleep states to the universal Divine presence, God or Ishvara within us, with the OM vibration as Ishvara's word. The inner guru or Ishvara is the transcendent consciousness behind deep sleep.

Modern Yoga teachings rarely examine the Yoga of the Four States, though it is one of the most important traditional meditation approaches. It has not been afforded its proper place in the world Yoga movement, which emphasizes styles of asana practice that keep us caught in physical reality. The new study of Yoga Nidra and new recognition of the power of pratyahara, however, is a movement in the direction of understanding the four states that is very helpful, and needs to be taken farther beyond any mere bodily or personal concerns.

The Yoga of the Four States affords all Yoga approaches greater power of transformation and can be used with each of these in a different way, according to the path and the individual following it. Yet its goal is Moksha or the liberation of Consciousness and Self-realization.

Recognizing the Self Within

The Purusha or higher Self is the inner consciousness that persists throughout the three states of waking, dream and deep sleep. Reaching that Purusha or Atmic state is entering into the transcendent fourth state, called Turiya, which literally means "the fourth." That is the state of liberation or supremacy, the Kaivalya or state of the supremacy of the Purusha that is the ultimate goal of Yoga practice.[5]

Unless we able to conquer the three lower states of waking, dream and deep sleep, we cannot access the true unitary Self-awareness beyond body and mind, in which alone is the liberation of the soul and union with the Supreme. This means that we must understand and deal with these three lower states, including the karmas, desires and imaginations involved with them, letting go of their attachments and releasing their pranic knots. These three states reflect the actions of the outer body, prana and mind that we must learn to go beyond.

The difficulty in pursuing this inner Yoga of Consciousness is that our meditation practice is usually limited to the waking state and focused on the waking mind and body, which is only the outer aspect of consciousness. We meditate to help deal with the problems of our personal lives and forget that meditation is meant to be a connection with the universal life. Such working on the surface cannot take us to the depths.

Even those who practice Yoga Nidra, which can be part of the Yoga of the Four States, usually look upon it in physical terms of its therapeutic value for the waking bodily self, not as a doorway beyond the outer world. They examine how it improves physiological and brain functions, as if it were another product of the physical body. Yoga Nidra holds the mystery of consciousness as its essence that we must examine deeply.

Controlling or calming the mind (nirodha) – such as mentioned in the *Yoga Sutras* as the methodology of Yoga – naturally occurs for everyone in the state of deep sleep.[6] This means that our inner being knows how to control and withdraw the mind and prana, and does it every day in waking and sleeping as a natural process. We must learn how to consciously access that natural internalization process, which can be revealed by patient and steady awareness.

All we need to do in order to achieve the highest goal of Yoga is to learn how to move through deep sleep with consciousness. Yet this process of dissolving the mind is not something we can accomplish by mere personal effort or by any activity of the mind. It is the same as our experience with going to sleep at night. We cannot force or think ourselves into the state of sleep; we must relax, let go and surrender in order to fall into it. It is a kind of self-forgetfulness, not a motivated activity. Sleep happens naturally as a biological process outside of our conscious control at a subconscious level. Yoga requires learning to reach this inner state of mergence at a higher conscious level, which similarly requires letting go of the mind and body-consciousness but in a deeper manner.

Chitta or Mind in *Yoga Sutras*

The mind in the general sense, or *chitta* in yogic thought as in the *Yoga Sutras*[7], which is the main focus and instrument of Yoga practice, is not merely the waking rational or personal mentality. Chitta includes all aspects of our personal consciousness through waking, dream and deep sleep. The *Yoga Sutras* recognizes sleep as one function of the chitta,[8] while vikalpa or imagination, another function, is connected to dream.[9]

In this regard, understanding and control of the dream and deep sleep states is more important for meditation than simply focusing on the waking mind and its psychological issues that have little relevance apart from the physical world. Chitta is the mind of dream and deep sleep as well, not just the mind of the waking state and its attempts to know the external world.

Chitta includes the reincarnating part of the mind that is latent behind the state of deep sleep. The deeper karmic compulsions that bind us to the Samsara of ignorance and rebirth are held in the subconscious awareness of deep sleep and can only be removed from there if we can shine the light of consciousness upon it. The activities of the waking mind have little effect upon the deeper subconscious, and sustain them in the background by continuing a limited ego consciousness. This is also because the deeper levels of the subconscious are not in the physical body or outer mind, but at a karmic level that is passed on from one birth to another.

Yet the ultimate goal of Yoga is to move beyond mind or chitta in all its aspects to pure Consciousness or Chit, which transcends all embodiment, and the witness to all the movements of the mind. *Chit is the Purusha or inner Self, while mind or chitta is part of Prakriti and external to our true nature.* True consciousness is beyond all aspects of the mind, which is but its instrument of expression.

Yoga of the Four States and the *Upanishads*

These four states of consciousness are examined in detail in the famous *Mandukya Upanishad*, the shortest but perhaps most important of the older classical *Upanishads*. In the *Mandukya*, the Yoga of the Four States is aligned with the Yoga of OM, the Divine word or cosmic sound vibration that projects the universe and sustains the vibration of pure Consciousness operating it. This fourfold Yoga of consciousness relates to OM and its four aspects, as the letters A, U, M and the vibration of dissolution. We will examine this entire *Upanishad* in detail later in the book.

The Yoga of the Four States is common in other classical *Upanishads* as well. The *Prashna Upanishad* carries much important information about the four states, including their connections with the different types of Prana.[10] The *Brihadaranyaka Upanishad,* one of the largest and oldest of these texts, addresses it prominently as well, showing us how to reach the state of pure unity and comprehend the non-duality of Atman and Brahman.[11]

The Yoga of the Four States is referred to in numerous places in Yoga and Vedanta teachings. Advaita or non-dualistic Vedanta is rooted in the teachings of the sage Gaudapada and his commentary, *Mandukya Karika*[12], on the *Mandukya Upanishad,* which includes his detailed discussion on the four states. The great Advaitic guru Shankaracharya wrote a detailed commentary (*Bhashya*) on the *Mandukya Karika,* which forms the basis of his profound teachings and his own special works on Advaita.[13] We will examine these teachings as well.

The Yoga of Consciousness has a profound traditional basis but we must remember that it is rooted in the movement of our life experience every day. It is not something merely philosophical or academic in its concerns. Each day provides us the opportunity to develop an understanding of the whole of life and consciousness. Each day contains the whole of time and a synopsis of our entire lives. We need to reclaim each day for our journey in consciousness for a higher awareness to emerge.

The Divine Self can arise within us like the Sun rises every single day, if we give it the space and silence to manifest with the roar of OM. This occurs when we learn to live within, discovering the entire universe inside us.

Our Four States of Consciousness

Consciousness is the very basis of our existence, abiding as a steady inner light illuminating the ongoing changes of our lives. It holds the magic, wonder and delight that pervades the universe, its myriad forces and creatures. We are by nature conscious beings working through the instrumentalities of body and mind. We are neither bodies, nor minds, but provide their guiding and motivational forces through our inner awareness. We have the potential to exist without body or mind in the space of consciousness, with no loss of our true nature.

Our current physical incarnation is but one of many lives, gathering experience in our different sojourns through the outer worlds of time and space. Our current human life is but a stage on these travels, not our true existence. Consciousness endows us with a sense of self, feeling and knowing, out of which body and mind function and would be lifeless without it. Pure consciousness is the very core of our being, the real person within us, for whom each life is but one of its many expressions.

Yet the essence of our consciousness is unknown to our ordinary mentality. We are so busy projecting our awareness into the external world that we have forgotten its origins deep inside us. We are trapped in a bodily image of ourselves that shadows our inner essence of light and bliss. Our transient physical lives mask our inner connection with the eternal, leaving us caught in an endless stream of action and reaction, the Samsara or wheel of illusion of Vedantic philosophy.

The result of this external vision is that we fall into ignorance, desire, and sorrow, driven by external compulsions rather than by internal knowing. We remain at the turbulent surface of our being and fail to note the calm depths within. We pursue happiness in the dense material world that is hard to achieve and even harder to hold, failing to recognize the subtle bliss that is our true nature.

Our lives hold the mystery of a background play of awareness, its concealment and unfoldment. Exploring that inner secret should be our most important endeavor, not simply running after outer enjoyments. We should carefully examine our own minds, not just the external world, and learn the wonders that dwell within us. Most importantly, we should learn the profound implications of our daily movement of consciousness through waking and sleep that connects us to the underlying powers of the universal life. This is the key to inner transformation, which brings about a bliss far more exalting than any drug or media experience.

Our Daily Pilgrimage through Consciousness

Let us provide an overview of the four states of consciousness as preliminary to their detailed exploration. We have four states of consciousness possible as human beings. These are different in nature, energy and function.

First are the three ordinary states of waking, dream and deep sleep that are well known to us and experienced daily by all. Then there is an ever-wakeful transcendent fourth state known as *Turiya*, which we only have intimations of. Although we do not directly know the fourth state, we all have a sense of a higher and more enduring reality beyond our outer personal lives.

Vedic thought has extensively explored this mystery of these four states of consciousness. It presents a clear system for understanding their levels of reality and a practical means for transcending their limitations. This movement in consciousness is the daily "Yoga of the Four States", as waking, dream, deep sleep and the ever-aware fourth state.

Consciousness is not a mere metaphysical concern of little practical relevance. Consciousness is our most powerful daily experience, the very fabric of our lives. The chemicals and hormones of the body could not function without the energy and light of awareness. The physical world is but a shadow of a higher consciousness beyond physical matter. Consciousness is not a mere by-product of bodily activities. On the contrary, bodily activities are but a densification of the light of consciousness.

Each day for us is a movement through the three states of waking, dream, and deep sleep in which our awareness withdraws in order to rise again. Ordinarily we are concerned only with the waking state and its powerful physical demands, but dream and deep sleep also have their value, identity, and experience that have a profound impact on all that we do, from health to spirituality.

We do not dwell in a uniform state of consciousness throughout the day and night, though we downplay these variations in self-perception. The nature of our consciousness changes radically through the states of waking, dream, and deep sleep. Along with this, the movement of our life force and perception of the world changes profoundly, including our sense of who we are.

We are primarily engrossed in the waking state, busily engaged in its projects, to the exclusion of even considering the other two states. We do experience dreams both beautiful and frightening that can enthrall or disturb us. Some of us have active and colorful dream lives and find a greater comfort being asleep than awake. Yet we treat dream as an interesting sideshow to the more solid waking lives. Deep sleep remains an obscure mystery that we seldom address or give importance to. Yet this daily movement of consciousness continues constantly, carrying our life experience like a great river from birth to death and beyond.

Our Objective World of the Waking State

The waking state forms our objective world, the world of externally based verifiable experience. It is the material world that we can palpably experience through the five senses and physical body, which exhibits regularity, stability and certainty. We share this waking world with other people and work together within it as part of a particular society and culture. The waking state links us to nature and other creatures and the vastness of Mother Earth. We regard it as our home or base, though it is only a part of our lives.

The waking state reveals a vivid external world through an outer consciousness of the five senses whose importance cannot be denied. It appears steady and solid and can be experienced objectively by all of us, at least for a time. We can compare and correlate waking experiences and construct a verifiable physical reality, with definite laws, processes and connections. Even from a spiritual or yogic standpoint, we must recognize the waking world as the primary realm of karma, where we both experience the results of our karmas and create new karmas to chart our future.

Yet waking experience contains many variations relative to our shifting attention span, from moments of mental clarity to periods of distraction and dullness. The nature of physical reality outwardly has many fluctuations, uncertainties and is ultimately transient through the movement of the days and years. Physical reality ends up being hardly as substantial as it initially appears to be, and our personal presence within it is even less certain. We are but visitors in the waking world, though that visit may constitute a lifetime.

The Subjective World of Dream

The dream state is our subjective world of imagination born of the darkness of sleep. Our dreams usually reflect waking experiences and memories but can extend to a creative or artistic vision beyond waking reality, or to a deeper spiritual vision. Dreams are largely personal but can overlap with the dreams of other people, particularly those that we sleep with, moving into dream worlds of collective experience. In dream each one of us creates his or her own reality according to our thoughts. Our thoughts that are concealed behind waking experiences gain their own theater of expression.

The dream state reflects an inner imaginative consciousness that is dramatic and colorful, changes rapidly, and is subjective in nature. In dreams we create our own personal reality with its own sense of time and space, but with little seeming lasting effects on our outer lives. Our dreams lack continuity overall, though we do have certain dream realms that we can regularly experience.

Ordinarily we take the dream world to be unreal, as different from the solid reality of the waking world. Yet dreams have their beauty and fascination as well. As we become more inwardly aware, our dream world can gain a deeper meaning and a greater consistency. It can become a reality of its own, and a place of subtle learning and experience. Nature in the dream state does not come to an end but gains a subtle vibrancy as the beauty and magic of dream worlds and dream experiences.

The State of Mergence of Deep Sleep

The deep sleep state constitutes the foundational state of mergence that is the culmination of the sleep state that begins with dream. It is much more mysterious and indefinable than the other two states of waking and dream that mirror each other. Deep sleep has no body, mind, form or changing images and experiences. It is a state of withdrawal and emptiness but does possess a special power of renewal that supports an ability to function in the other two states.

Deep sleep withdraws us into a mass of unmanifest consciousness, in which everything else is obscured and brought back into a seed form. Deep sleep is easy to overlook but we cannot have any happiness or wellbeing without it. It is the ultimate state of peace that we look forward to when we go to sleep every night. It is like returning home, though to a mysterious forgotten abode. As the least acknowledged of the three states, it is easy to overlook its importance, power or potentials.

The Fourth State of Transcendence

Beyond these three ordinary states, yet more hidden and mysterious, endures the potential for an ever-wakeful awareness not subject to any daily fluctuations – the transcendent fourth or Turiya in yogic thought. The state of transcendence or Turiya lies far beyond the usual three states but is ever present behind them, with each of the other three states manifesting some of its qualities. The transcendent state holds the wakefulness in the waking state, the creative imagination in the dream state, and the peace and rest in the deep sleep state. From this transcendent light we gain an intuition of unity consciousness, the divine, the eternal, infinite and universal.

Discovering Turiya is the goal of higher Yoga practices necessary to take us beyond time and death. Turiya is where the real secret of existence dwells but to unravel it we must search it out with full determination, working through the other three states first in a consistent manner. *Though this state is called the fourth relative to the other three, it is the state of unity consciousness that underlies and transcends them. As such it is beyond all numerical classification.*

Some yogis propose a fifth state of *Turiyatita* (beyond the fourth) in which the awareness of the fourth state is continual throughout the day. It consists of abidance in the state of the witness or pure consciousness underlying all states of mind. Others consider this fifth state as an extension of the fourth state and do not mention it. Some extend these states to seven, but the higher four are different levels or aspects of the same unitary reality of the fourth state in their individual and cosmic dimensions.

Our Four Selves and Four Realms of Experience

Each of these four states has its unique self, world and experience. We tend to overlook our other three selves in a fixation on physical reality and the waking state but they have their own existence as well.

- The Self of the Waking State and the Waking World
- The Self of the Dream State and the Dream World
- The Self of the Deep Sleep State and the Deep Sleep State World
- The Transcendent Self and the Absolute beyond all manifestation

Usually we are only aware of the waking self, which constitutes our ordinary ego identity that we wrongly regard as our real self. We are not aware of the other selves or states of consciousness except as shadows of the waking self. We do not know how to communicate with the selves of dream and deep sleep, or to integrate our waking self-awareness with them. We are only vaguely and transiently aware of the dream world, and have almost no awareness of the deep sleep realm.

The waking self undergoes many changes throughout the aging process and our life experience. The dream self varies in different dreams, though there is some unity or commonality to our dream self and its spectrum of experiences. It is hard to call the self of deep sleep a self, as it has no real corresponding world of experience. But it is a condition of awareness. The fourth or transcendent Self is our true nature of which the other three are but phases or manifestations.

We must learn to become aware of all aspects of Self and world, extending to our true Self beyond body and mind, waking and sleep. This is what Yoga and Self-realization based spirituality is all about. We must learn to manifest our full potential in consciousness that is universal. Each of these four aspects of ourselves has corresponding connections with similar aspects in the universe as a whole.

The Yogas of the Four States

A true integral Yoga will practice Yoga on all four levels and in all four states, linking them together. This is only possible when we are connected to the fourth level of unity that underlies the other three states. Different Yoga attitudes and practices are recommended relative to the four states as well as practices in common to promote a continuous awareness through them.

- The Yoga of the Waking State for cultivating true wakefulness

- The Yoga of the Dream State for cultivating creative vision
- The Yoga of Deep Sleep for cultivating inner peace
- The Yoga of Transcendence for direct Self-realization through pure awareness

Our true Self is not merely the self of the waking state identified with the physical body. It is our true nature behind and beyond all the states of waking, dream and deep sleep. It is important that we are aware of all aspects of our self and consciousness, waking, dream, deep sleep and beyond as different aspects of who we are as a spiritual being. Each has its own place and validity, its own practices and place for our ultimate wellbeing.

Your physical self is at best one quarter of who you are, and though the most known to you, is the most outward and superficial aspect of your being, the most caught in illusory appearances and ignorance. Do not let its compulsions and demands block you from experiencing the deeper states of your consciousness and your vast potentials within them.

Do not give all your attention to the waking state and its complications. Do not consider your waking achievements to be the true purpose and meaning of your existence. Keep your attention active in dream and deep sleep as well, where there is a greater lightness and freedom of being.

Remember to honor all the different levels and aspects of your awareness, not just the realm of the senses. That is the only way to wholeness and the full integration of your being. *You are the one who wakes in the waking state, dreams in the dream state, gets renewed in deep sleep, but ever witnesses all these three states from a standpoint of eternity beyond.*

Waking perception, creative intelligence, and lasting inner peace are but three facets of your deeper consciousness beyond body and mind. You can discover that the entire universe dwells within you and that you dwell within the entire universe, which exists on many levels and dimensions, within and without. We will explore these different Yogas of the Four States in the upcoming chapters, including both their unique features and their interconnections.

Mind and Prana in the Four States

Our Biological Clock

Our lives are driven and timed by an extraordinary internal biological clock that governs and the entire movement of our lives. Our biological clock regulates our activities throughout the day and the entire aging process. Yet it does not only affect us at physical level but also reflects an inner development in consciousness that few understand. Our biological rhythms are not defined merely by outer energies but are ultimately connected to inner powers of eternity, from which alone do we gain a capacity to renew both body and mind.

Our biological clock is connected to the cycles of nature and to cosmic time at a deep level. It reflects the movement of the sun outwardly, as we naturally tend to wake up by the morning sunlight and go to sleep at night after the sun has set. At an inner level, this biological clock is defined by prana and measured by the breath.

During each day, according to ancient yogic texts,[14] we have 21,600 breaths, or about one every four seconds, with 360 breaths every 24 minutes or 1/60th of a day, a number like the days of the year. Our prana is linked to the cosmic prana through the sun. Our organic time is linked to the rhythms of the universe. The Earth in its daily rotations and yearly revolutions absorbs solar energy, differing in warmth and prana through the seasons.

The mind, holding our thoughts and emotions, moves along

with the breath, and shares its rhythms and fluctuations, both moment by moment and by day and night. The breath carries our thoughts inward on inhalation and externalizes them on exhalation through speech. During sleep our prana turns within us along with the mind to a withdrawn state of minimal functioning.

In the state of deep sleep, our biological clock is reset for another day. Without this inner reset, it will continue to run into a state of entropy, as its basic durational power is only around sixteen hours, after which we begin to feel sleepy and tired. If we continue to be active too long without sleep, our entire energy field will collapse, reducing our mental power as well.

Of course, modern life-styles and technology have removed us very far from the organic time cycles of nature. We measure time as defined by society more so than by nature, with mechanical clocks and their numerical precision and the use of artificial lights and electronically driven forms of stimulation. We try to stay up longer at night and resist the natural biological urge to rest. Eventually we must compromise with our biological rhythms or proper sleep will be denied to us, and our physiological and psychological functions will be disturbed.

Our artificial lives are rooted in an artificial sense of time, which endows us with an artificial sense of identity. Our clock time is mechanical and brings an artificial rhythm into our lives.

The fact as determined by our biological clock is that we live one day at a time, with each day providing a new potential for experience that is unique and self-contained. Our body and mind continue day after day but undergo subtle changes and alterations, mainly during sleep. *Our lives are not a continual forward movement in time but modulated or broken by the fluctuations of day and night.*

Our biological clock speeds up and slows down, from phases of activity to those of rest. It is cyclical rather than progressive in terms of development. Our timeline is not linear but a spiral through the cycles of the days and years, extending into different incarnations.

Our consciousness returns to an unmanifest state every night during sleep and then reemerges in the morning for another day, like a daily death and rebirth. We forget this fact of our daily withdrawal from physical reality in an obsession with our physical existence, as if there were a continuous existence of the physical personality, which is not really the case. Our physical personality lives in a set of flashes day by day that we mentally connect and perceive as a continual existence. Yet that is but a blurred perception and not a fact.

Deeper forces of consciousness and eternity embrace us in our daily life-cycles, connecting us to a profound Self-awareness beyond the ego. The waking mind is but the shadow of a deeper hidden light. It is not a conscious wakefulness but a shifting connection to the vibrant world of the five senses on the outside that keeps us awake by constantly changing stimuli. If we close the senses off even during the day, our tendency is to fall asleep.

Similarly, our spiritual development proceeds one day at a time, with each day offering us a new opportunity for growth, transformation and deeper realization of our inner being. We must learn to embrace the uniqueness and transforming power of each single day, which has its own special characteristics, constituting its own world and duration. Then each day will be an experience of wonder for us.

Each new day should have a certain freshness for both body

and mind, along with new hope and aspiration, not merely drudgery to face another difficult challenge. Once we recognize that we return to the Divine in sleep, each day will be a further embrace of our Divine potentials, a manifestation of the Divine both within us and in our outer expression.

Mind, Prana and Speech in the Four States

The mind undergoes major changes in the three states of waking, dream and deep sleep. In the waking state, the mind is connected to the physical senses. In dream, it dwells in its own world of imagination. In deep sleep, it is merged into a state of background blank awareness.

Our prana or vital force undergoes the same type of changes as the mind. Our prana is active outwardly during the day through the physical body, starting after we wake up in the morning. As we fall asleep, our prana turns within, with the outer mind and cognitive senses suspended from action along with the motor organs. Our waking life and activity is put into abeyance. Yet our prana continues to light up the mind with various dream experiences in a dream body. In deep sleep, prana merges into a unitary state. Our breath becomes deeper and it is more difficult to wake us up. Our mental activities come to an end.

Similarly, our speech or inner sound energy, our main power of expression, changes through these three daily states. In the waking state, audible speech is our primary activity through the vocal organs, generally interacting with other people, but also maintaining an internal voice in our minds. In the dream state, speech is connected with the imagination of the mind, and no longer depends upon the physical vocal organs but does continue its own expression. In deep sleep, speech is merged into a vibration of silence.

In the waking state, both mind and prana are active outwardly. The mind is caught in the dualistic currents connected to the external world; attraction and repulsion, like and dislike, pleasure and pain, and love and hate. Our prana similarly is caught in the dualistic currents of inhalation and exhalation, sensation and action, and the movement of energy on the right and left sides of the body. Our speech patterns also reflect the dualities of the mind, with friendly or unfriendly statements, expressions of like and dislike, love and hate.

In the dream state, the mind is withdrawn and our prana also turns within. Our inner mind comes forth with its luminous dreams and powers to radically alter time-space experiences. We also experience a subtler non-physical prana that projects a changeable dream body according to the thoughts of the mind. Speech is merged into the mind and its reactions.

In deep sleep, the mind merges into a state of latency and ceases to function. The body is upheld by prana, which sustains it from its seed level.[15] We experience a natural deep pratyahara, or sensory withdrawal, in which all our faculties return to their core energy. Speech is withdrawn into a restful vibration.

In the fourth state of Turiya – for those who are able to experience it through meditation – prana and mind are merged within a deeper consciousness. One discovers the state of pure awareness beyond the mind. The mind ceases to make any movements of its own, functioning only as an instrument of unitary consciousness. To reach that fourth state, we must give up identification with the body, and remove the knot of prana that connects us to it through the navel center. At that higher level we can connect to the universal Prana, Brahman, and the universal speech, the cosmic sound vibration OM.

Mind and the Four States

We can summarize the four levels of the mind as below:

- Waking Mind - resting upon sensory activity, dominated by the five cognitive senses of hearing, touch, sight, taste and smell that connect us to the external physical world.
- Dream Mind - resting upon imagination primarily rooted in memory. Envisions its own world as well as our interaction within it. Sensory inputs are simulated by the mind.
- Merged Mind in Deep Sleep - in which the mind is withdrawn into its seed state of not knowing, ignorance or avidya. Only one root sense of life remains.
- Beyond the mind or Pure Consciousness state, the transcendent fourth, which is that of the Universal Self. This provides us access to higher states of awareness, or Self-realization.

Prana and the Four States

The four states of Prana can be summarized as follows.

- Waking Prana - connected to the motor organs and outer physical activity.
- Dream Prana – connected to the mind alone, with only residual body motions.
- Deep Sleep or Merged Prana – body in a state of deep rest, suspended animation as it were.
- Transcendent, Unitary or Immortal Prana beyond the body and mind. Prana freely moves beyond the body and is connected to the universal Self, Brahman.

Speech and the Four States

Speech has the same four variations.

- Waking Speech through the vocal organs.
- Dream Speech through the mind.
- Merged Speech through an inner silence.
- Transcendent speech connected to the Divine Word OM.

The location of consciousness relative to the body also changes in the four states:

- In the waking state, it is said that consciousness dwells in the eyes, specifically the right eye and the cognitive activities that it guides.
- In the dream state, it is said to dwell in the throat, where imagination functions.
- In deep sleep, it is said to dwell in the heart, meaning the deeper spiritual heart, not simply the physical or emotional heart.
- In the fourth state, it is also centered in the heart but consciously, not unconsciously as in deep sleep, which connects it to the infinite.

Four States and Three Bodies

The three states relate to the three bodies of the individual soul as gross, subtle and causal as explained in yogic texts. The fourth state is beyond all embodiment.

- **Waking State, Physical Body**

  The gross physical body is made up of the gross elements of earth, water, fire, air and space. It is sustained by food and drink and is active in the waking state.

- **Dream State, Subtle Astral Body**
  The subtle energy body is made up of the subtle elements or sensory components of sound, touch, sight, taste and smell, and is active in dream and inspiration.

- **Deep Sleep State, Formless Causal Body**
  Deep sleep is the causal state that is the basis and origin of waking and dreaming. It consists of the seed state of the elements, and is only accessed in sleep and samadhi.

Four States and Five Sheaths or Koshas

We can further correlate the three bodies with the five sheaths or koshas of yogic thought. The three bodies relate to five sheaths or koshas, with additional koshas between the physical and subtle bodies, and the subtle and causal bodies.

- Waking State and food (anna) sheath or *Annamaya Kosha*, corresponding to the physical body and its tissues and organs.

- Intermediate energy (prana) sheath or *Pranamaya Kosha*, links physical body and mind largely through the motor organs, active outwardly in waking and inwardly in dream.

- Dream State and mental (manas) sheath or *Manomaya kosha*, corresponding to imagination and sensory impressions.

- Intermediate intelligence (vijnana) sheath or *Vijnanamaya kosha*, links mind and bliss sheath, and provides deeper insight. Expressive in the dream state, this sheath is concentrated during deep sleep.

- Deep sleep and bliss (ananda) sheath or *Anandamaya kosha*, corresponding to an ability to find bliss or lasting happiness through our experience.

- Transcendent bodiless state as Being-Consciousness-Bliss Absolute or *Satchitananda*, connects to the universal reality.

Prana mediates between mind and body. Intelligence mediates between mind and bliss. In the waking state, the food sheath predominates and the other sheaths are in the background. In dream, the food sheath is withdrawn and the mental sheath prevails. In deep sleep, the mental sheath is withdrawn and the bliss sheath becomes active.

According to some Yogis we human beings have only developed to the level of the mind or Manomaya kosha. The other two higher koshas of Vijnana (intelligence) and Ananda (bliss) only function in us in a diminished manner through Manomaya kosha. They are only activated in the state of Samadhi, meaning that awareness in deep sleep also helps us develop these higher koshas as well as transcend them.

Healing and the Four States

Drawing our prana inwards is the essence of all deeper healing. In this regard, the merged prana of deep sleep has a special power to heal the waking and dream pranas, thereby healing both mind and body. The merged prana holds a special power of rejuvenation and emotional healing and supports positive health and longevity.

In deep sleep, modern science has discovered that the brain is able to remove toxins and negative patterns and energies from the brain cells. It enables us to reset the brain's equilibrium, which is very important in all psychological therapies. Without this restorative action of deep sleep, the brain will lack the freshness for another day and will quickly deteriorate. Deep sleep serves to sustain the immune system at both physical and psychological levels.

The deepest healing of the body comes from the awareness and prana underlying deep sleep. A yogi can access this inner power of prana and direct it through his hands or through his eyes, using it to guide or to heal others. A yogi can also instill that prana into an object of devotion, like a statue, picture, yantra or linga; and set up a temple or sacred site for all to benefit from and feel renewed by.

According to Ayurvedic medicine, deep sleep refreshes body and mind, sustaining a deeper vitality. It calms *Vata dosha*, the biological air humor. *Vata* is the force responsible for most diseases and for the aging process, and increases during agitation or depletion. Deep sleep also calms *Pitta dosha*, the fire energy, and cools our minds and emotions. Similarly deep sleep calms *Kapha dosha,* or watery entropy, and removes us from the outer realm of attachment and accumulation.

Deep sleep fortifies *Ojas*, the vital essence of all the tissues of the body and of the food that we eat. It nourishes *Tarpak Kapha* or the inner nectar that calms and nourishes the brain and nervous system. The deep sleep state is like the central axis of our vitality, returning to which restores our organic balance. It holds the deepest level of prana and sustains clarity of mind and power of attention.

Without proper deep sleep, the mind and prana, along with the doshas or biological humors – starting with Vata dosha, the core physiological motivating force – become imbalanced and cause a progressive breakdown in our organic functioning. Deep sleep balances the pranas and grounds us in a deeper vitality, without which our energy remains erratic and depleted. Without deep sleep our immunity, endurance and patience collapses, leading to collapse of body and mind.

The dream state also reflects our mental digestion or Agni of the mind, how we have digested the experiences of the given day and whatever other experiences it stimulates. Dreams help us understand how our digestive fire of the mind, the buddhi or higher power of discernment, is functioning. Toxic dreams show a toxic mental state and poor mental digestion leading to emotional unrest. Happy dreams show an ability to digest positive experiences, promoting inner peace.

Yet the highest power of mental digestion gives us clarity and wakefulness in the dream state and may not produce any dreams at all, or it may bring us inner visions beyond ordinary dreams. *You should note your dreams every day and see what they are telling you about your mental activity and your ability to digest your life experiences.* Undigested experiences create karma and attachment, conditioning the mind and keeping us bound to the world of duality.

Above all, we should learn to dwell in a clear and silent awareness that does not rest upon any thoughts or sensations, but can observe everything from a place of light. That is the best way to heal the mind. Such an inner space holds and develops the highest prana that can move beyond the body and mind into the infinite.

The Mystery of Sleep and Karma

We should always remain curious and continually investigate our daily movement in consciousness, like unraveling a great mystery or discovering a hidden secret. It is the most important factor in our entire lives, as it is also the mystery of death and rebirth, yet we easily overlook it. Notably, it is the basis of our karma and how we create our future.

This process of inner investigation begins with an examination of our own thoughts, their energies and implications. Each day of our lives is a new wonder and magic of experience, not simply outwardly in the ever-changing beauty of nature, but inwardly in what our deeper consciousness and perception can unfold behind the veils of the mind.

The Yoga of Consciousness is our natural Yoga that follows our daily development of awareness. Practicing it allows us to make every day into a transformative movement in inner awakening. By this movement, every moment of the day can provide a special Yoga and meditation insight. Our daily Yoga practice should occur throughout the natural processes of waking and sleep. It should not just follow certain routine times of the day, timed Yoga classes or fixed practices. It should be a full Yoga of consciousness, with its own creative dynamic, and not just an activity of body and mind.

Yet most of us, even on the spiritual path, afford little importance to our daily cycle of consciousness. We are firmly dedicated to the waking reality and its continuity over time. Our attention is focused on the external world and the waking actions of the physical body, for which all else is but a shadow.

Our primary concern is our outer work in the material world that we get paid for, after which we may move into a phase of relaxation if we have completed our obligations for the day.

For us, sleep is but a temporary suspension from a more important waking reality, with its pressing tasks, duties, demands, pleasures and engagements. We tend to dislike sleep as an interruption from a more engaging waking world. We may regard sleep as a biological necessity but do not afford it a small degree of the significance we afford to the waking state. *We must recognize that our main spiritual work actually begins when we fall asleep.* If we lose our inner awareness when we fall asleep, it means that we have not developed it properly during waking hours.

The waking self has its counterparts as dream and deep sleep selves, which have their own identities, actions and purposes that are sometimes different than its. Our waking ego dominates the dream self and deep sleep self, which we do not seek to develop in their own right.

To truly awaken in consciousness rather than just to be awake during the day, our waking ego must be subordinated to a deeper soul identity that is not limited to our current body or physical incarnation. We must remember our greater soul purpose in life is to develop a higher awareness, not simply to gain enjoyments or possessions externally that we must eventually lose anyway. We must remember that we have had many previous waking lives among the dreams of our immortal soul.

The problem is that we identify ourselves with the waking self and consider the dream and sleep states only to be only a biological rest within the larger scope of our waking reality. This keeps our consciousness confined to the outer world, the physical body and the realm of the senses. We fail to develop an enduring awareness and are content with spurts of attention off and on during our daily interactions with the waking world. This severely limits how efficacious our Yoga and meditation practices can be.

We ignore the daily shift of states of consciousness from waking to sleep as inconsequential to our true reality. We fail to understand how we can use these shifts to raise our awareness to a higher level beyond the body and ego. We emphasize making changes in our waking lives and physical bodies, and do not realize that the shifts of states of our consciousness to dream and deep sleep can grant greater connections to higher worlds and planes of consciousness.

The self that wakes up in the morning is never exactly the same as the self that goes to sleep at night. Dream and deep sleep introduce subtle changes in body, mind and prana that can trigger major changes in our life and consciousness, including karmic changes and shifts in perception. The keys to higher awareness and spiritual development reside as much in the dream and the deep sleep states as in the waking state. Sleep both hides the ignorance of our personal lives and provides a doorway to move beyond it to the true world of perpetual light.

Sleep and the Home

Most of us define our homes as the place where we sleep, reflecting sleep as defining our identity. The bedroom is the most intimate room in the house. We all look forward to going home and having a good night's rest after a hectic day or after having traveled away and returned. Having no home or place to sleep of our own is a great trauma. Establishing a home or place of rest is the foundation of our sense of wellbeing. Sleeping in the same place affords us a certain inner contentment and continuity of existence.

Yet it is not just a question of a house, room or physical home. Sleep takes us back to our spiritual home, the Divine energy and consciousness through which deep sleep renews us. We all sense that benefic power in sleep. When we have difficulties in life, we all wish to return to the quiet and rest of our homes, wherein we can shut the outer world off, be ourselves, relax, let go and have a good sleep.

We are happy to go to sleep because we recognize that sleep brings us a natural state of peace and happiness in which we can let all the cares and worries of the world fade away. Whether one is a beggar or a king, sleep is the same for everyone. The peace of deep sleep helps us understand the peace inherent in our deeper consciousness. Yet it is not enough to rest in our outer home, we must learn to rest in our inner home, which is the core awareness within the spiritual heart. Our true home is beyond the state of deep sleep, in the ever wakeful Divine awareness connected to the hearts of all.

Why Do We Sleep?

We know the biological reasons for sleeping – a biological necessity to renew our vitality – and may consider that sufficient to explain why we sleep. Yoga teaches us that there are additional spiritual reasons for sleep that are more important. These reasons reflect our connection to a greater reality beyond the physical world.

According to Yoga, the waking state and the physical life is not our natural state of being. Physical life is something temporary, artificial and constructed as it were, neither self-existent nor intrinsic. It is a transient realm of experience that we only pass through for a time, and cannot permanently reside in. This conclusion is quite reasonable if we look at the issue carefully.

It is not just a question of the transience of our lives from birth to death. Our physical life is ever changing, not still even for a moment. Yet it is also shrouded in darkness. We are ignorant of our reality or existence before birth and after death – and most importantly every day during sleep. Our physical life is not inherent or enduring but fragile and uncertain. For example, fire always burns, as that is its nature. We cannot separate fire from its burning quality. Unlike the burning quality, which is always present with fire, life is not always present in the body. It exists only under special circumstances according to complex sustaining processes at biological and social levels.

To maintain a physical life we must eat, drink, breathe, move and interact with the world in various ways, which can be very demanding to fulfill. Should any of these processes become disrupted or deficient, we may fall ill or suffer harm. Should they be obstructed long term, we may die. Yet even if we maintain our life processes at an optimal level, we still eventually age and die. Death is inherent in the body and in physical matter. The soul and its life-force is merely a guest in the physical body – a temporary configuration relying upon a precise alignment of numerous complex factors.

The physical body is not a homogeneous entity. It is a conglomeration of various tissues, organs, fluids, energies and processes that have a limited ability to endure or stay together. Life creates a certain friction that eventually wears the body out, and its different components return to their natural state in the material world, going back to the earth and the material substances they derive from.

This means that waking life is not a fact of being; it is a process of change and becoming that has its ups and downs, and must ultimately come to an end. *Life has another home and native abode, where unlike in physical reality, it does not have to struggle hard to exist or endure.*

Unlike this dense physical reality, where it is obstructed and made dull by the heaviness of the physical body and the fluids of the brain, mind too has another home and native abode. Sleep is the shadow of waking life, which like death calls its reality into question. It tells us that our waking life and its activity is limited, unable to endure continuously even for a day.

According to Yoga there is a deeper spiritual reason for sleep. Sleep allows us to temporarily withdraw from physical reality in order to return the higher levels of being where our energy and consciousness can be renewed, not merely the body. This renewal allows us to come back to physical reality and live longer to fulfill our karma. Sleep is our natural samadhi or connection to cosmic consciousness. Sleep teaches us that we are not physical beings, and reminds us that we have a deeper Self beyond body and mind, and an eternal reality beyond physical time.

Deep Sleep and Death

Along with the mystery of deep sleep is the related mystery of death. Both sleep and death involve the suspension of our physical body and mind; sleep daily and temporarily, death permanently. Dream and deep sleep intimate the secrets of death and after death states, following the same process as death and rebirth in a reduced manner. If we learn the Yoga of sleep, we can also learn the Yoga of death and be able to use the moment of death as a point of transformation into the timeless, taking us beyond all death and sorrow.

We are not afraid of sleep, though we forget our minds and bodily identities in the process. Similarly, we should not be afraid of death. Death can only reveal our own deathless reality if we are prepared for it in our awareness. We can easily cast off the body and mind for shorter or longer periods and not lose our true Self that is inherently beyond them. The shorter letting go of body and mind is sleep; the longer letting go is death. The two are not as fundamentally different as we may think.

Deep meditation draws us into a state of withdrawal from the outer world, much like deep sleep and death. It requires a suspension of the mind and letting go of attachments to the world of time. One forgets one's personal identity and the details of the outer world, however important these may be. One gives up the mind and its outer knowledge and rests in the pure Self-knowing that is the nature of universal consciousness. Freedom from body and mind means freedom from action, pain, emotional fluctuations and ignorance. Such a state is not death but inner peace. We must learn how to use such states of inner withdrawal to develop our potential for Self-realization.

Karma and the Four States

Deep sleep forms the background lack of Self-awareness out of which the movement of karma occurs, holding a primordial ignorance and not knowing that causes karma to bind us. *Karma is nothing but action done in a state of ignorance, which means action circumscribed by the shadow of deep sleep.*

We live in the shadow of deep sleep even in the waking state, as our minds remain dominated by subconscious patterns rooted in the sleep state that we seldom question. Our karmic patterns or samskaras remain latent in deep sleep and manifest during waking hours. Until their roots in deep sleep are removed through the light of awareness, they will continue to influence us.

Karma does not arise from conscious action born of Self-awareness. Karma is a reactive process born of conditioning by the external world, a kind of mental compulsion. In other words, karma is something that we create only when we are spiritually ignorant and distracted in our minds, not when we are fully aware in our true nature. These karmic patterns affect us from the subconscious, circumventing reason and intelligence that are surface parts of the same mind and dominated by the same energies.

All action done without removing the root ignorance of deep sleep inevitably creates karma, which means we are caught in a limited awareness and conditioned responses. When we move into the fourth state of pure Consciousness, we naturally transcend all karmas, freeing ourselves from the shackles of time and space by letting go of the mind. Without attachment to the mind and its memories, karma cannot affect us.

- In the waking state, we create our primary karmas. The waking state, we could say, is the karmic state and constitutes our karmic reality where we can directly experience the results of our karmas.

- In dream, we experience the happiness or sorrow that forms the residue of our waking karmas. The subtle energy forms underlying our karmas continue in dream.

- In deep sleep, our karmas are held in reserve for future expression. Deep sleep is the root of karma, which is action bound by ignorance and compulsion.

- Turiya as the ever transcendent fourth state removes the ignorance from which karmas can arise, freeing us from karma and its limitations.

In your true nature as pure consciousness you are not a doer or performer of any action whatsoever. Action arises only from a connection with our instruments of mind, senses and body, which is circumstantial in nature. Action is not our intrinsic nature, which is peaceful awareness, but is transient and episodic in its movement. Many periods occur during the day when we are not active outwardly, yet we do not lose ourselves. In deep sleep, we touch upon the happiness and peace of this natural higher state of non-doing. We must be more conscious of the power of non-doing and learn to abide in our inner being, with action as something we perform as required but not defining what we are. Being itself has the highest power of transformation more so than any outer activity. Once we realize this we can move beyond all karmic limitations.

Yoga of the Four States and Other People

Just as we ordinarily look at ourselves according to our waking reality, we do the same for the people that we come into contact with. We look at others in terms of their waking reality, which occurs when we actively are engaged with them in the outer world. This is only natural as it is only in the waking state that we can clearly experience other people as separate beings.

Yet we should remember that each person and each creature undergoes the same states of consciousness as we do. When we sleep with or nearby others, we can connect at an energetic level to their dream and deep sleep selves as well.

When you look at other people, try to remember that they are also much more than their waking selves and their physical identity that you normally interact with. When we see another person's appearance in the waking world, we do not necessarily know what is going on in their minds and hearts. Operating the body and mind is an inner person not bound by name and form. Each person also merges back into deep sleep and the underlying primal reality every day, becoming one with all existence at an inner level, though not understanding the process.

While we are physically separate in our waking lives, we are all one in the state of deep sleep. When we reach the Fourth State of Turiya we become consciously one with all, and go beyond all bodily limitation and separations in consciousness. We discover that the entire universe dwells within us.

Our Daily Journey through the Four States of Consciousness

Each day of our lives is a journey in consciousness, which is also a journey into and out of ignorance. This is our *Jiva Yatra* or "soul journey" from the darkness of ego consciousness to the light of universal awareness, of which each day is a step in this long process.

Each night during sleep we return into the ground of our being or Divine essence for renewal, only to emerge again into an outer ego and body awareness every morning. We wake to the outer world but forget where we truly came from, falling from an inner domain of true awareness into an ignorance and sleep that constitutes our waking reality. Our bodily waking state is a spiritual veiling and a spiritual sleep. We forget our pure divine origin and essence and get caught in personal, physical and social compulsions and their endless complications, agitations and antagonisms. It is a journey into sorrow perhaps more than anything.

Our deeper soul journey is a movement through the states of consciousness of waking dream and deep sleep. Our ordinary personal self-consciousness arises and is active in the waking state. Our dream consciousness arises and is active in the dream state. And our deep sleep consciousness prevails in the deep sleep state. Yet underlying all three states is a growing light of awareness slowly struggling to emerge overall.

Our lives center on the waking state as the true reality. This is the automatic and accepted fact of our thought and behavior, much of which is rooted in physical, biological and social compulsions.

Even if we try to work with our dream and deep sleep states, it is for the benefit of the waking personality. Modern science and medicine explores dream and sleep only from the standpoint of the waking state and their physical implications. It does not afford them any independent reality of their own or any connection with realities beyond the physical.

Our waking life experience is reflected in the dream state, which is dominated by memory based fantasies. It is withdrawn back into its core in deep sleep. Because the sleep state is shorter and less action oriented than waking, we neglect its importance, though we know that good sleep is necessary for health and wellbeing in our physical lives. Yet sleep is also a doorway to other worlds, other states of consciousness, and other lives of our soul. Many so-called primitive and traditional people know this, but we moderns have forgotten it in an obsession with the world of technology as our civilizational obsession.

The Yoga of the Day and Night

Each day and night is a Yoga of waking and sleep for the soul. We must carefully understand how our consciousness is affected by these daily rhythms and how we can use them for inner transformation. Waking and sleeping form an expansion and contraction of consciousness. Yet they do not occur only as a daily cycle; to some degree they occur at different intervals throughout the day. Ultimately, phases like day and night happen at every moment in time, as the very breath of awareness, in its inhalation and exhalation, expansion and contraction. We have fluctuating moments of greater and lesser awareness throughout the day, of looking to the outside and turning within.

Our Yoga of the day, or daily routine, consists of our regular daily activities, which should aim at promoting a higher awareness and further the aim of our soul to connect to its cosmic reality. The Yoga of the day is rooted in outer action, which is best made into Karma Yoga, an offering to the Divine awareness within us. This occurs when we do not forget the inner light out of which outer action occurs. Without outer action to engage us, we naturally retreat inward from the waking world, either into fantasy or contemplation, as is our state of spiritual evolution. We should aim to be grounded in a constant meditative state.

Our Yoga of the night is a period of inactivity in which we move within and touch our hidden origins. The night is perhaps more suitable for Jnana Yoga and Bhakti Yoga, the Yogas of knowledge and devotion, which depend upon introspection and are easily disturbed by the active needs of the day. This Yoga of the night should begin at least two hours before we actually go to sleep, so that we can settle into it before drifting off into the dream state. It should continue after we wake up early in the morning for at least another hour, so that we can draw its energies in for the waking day.

We should carefully follow nature's rhythms of activity and repose and adjust to them, performing our appropriate work during the day, and taking the necessary rest and inner immersion at night. Day is much like exhalation for the soul and night is much like inhalation, with its energies moving out and moving in. Yet even during waking activity we can remain centered in our inner being, holding an inner peace in outer action by working according to an inner focus.

Eventually we must learn to merge these two currents of waking and sleeping and make them simultaneous – maintaining the wakeful observation of the waking state during sleep, and the restful peace of sleep in the waking state as an ongoing state of awareness. Then our soul will reach its journey's culmination, with its origin and end, its goal and fulfillment at every moment.

The ancient *Vedas* speak of the movement of day and night, dawn and dusk as our natural ritual or sacrifice (yajna), the sacred dance of awareness. These alternating dualistic currents of time teach the soul the Divine secrets of its own being and of the universe as a whole. Our own inner awareness is the Divine fire nurtured by these dualistic rhythms of light and dark. Our inner sacrifice consists of maintaining an inner flame of awareness throughout all the days and nights that constitute our lives by offering all that we experience into it. That inner flame of awareness alone can link our days into the spiraling flame of eternity.

Deep Sleep, the Greatest Mystery

The root of our human incarnation dwells in the state of deep sleep, in which we return to the divine source of our being, though unknowingly. In deep sleep we go back to the inner flame in which our energy and awareness get cleansed and vitalized for another day. But this experience in deep sleep is masked by the deep ignorance and forgetfulness of Maya, the illusion of the world.

This state of deep sleep is the *Mula-avidya* or "root ignorance" underlying our lives according to Vedantic thought. It presents the primary barrier to any higher consciousness or inner light. It is a darkness or unknowing at the core of the mind that conceals the greater reality of universal consciousness within us. Yet deep sleep is also potentially the main doorway to the liberation of consciousness, but only if we learn to examine it, understand it, and move through and beyond it.

Unless we learn to transcend the state of deep sleep through a higher awareness, we will remain bound by karma and desire, birth and death. We will live in the shadow of darkness and unreality, which is an inability to see beyond the darkness of deep sleep to the inner light of truth.

Deep sleep is not just a biological phenomenon but also a spiritual limitation, a boundary or barrier, often a closed door, between the inner and outer worlds. It is the core mystery of our existence. Unless we learn to awaken from this primordial darkness of deep sleep, we will not know our true cosmic reality. We must learn how to rend its veil asunder with the sword of discernment born of enduring meditation. This reminds us of a famous Vedic prayer that comes from the *Upanishads*.

> Asato mā sadgamaya
> Tamaso mā jyotirgamaya
> Mṛtyor mā amṛtam gamaya
>
> Lead me from non-being to being
> Lead me from darkness to light
> Lead me from death to immortality[16]

This movement from deep sleep to pure consciousness is a movement from inner darkness to inner light. Non-being, darkness and death are the nature of our consciousness on this side of deep sleep, under its shadow. Being, light, and immortality arise once we cross over deep sleep into ever-wakeful awareness, the inner light. *Crossing over death is not possible without crossing over deep sleep.* That is the alchemical journey of the soul from mortality to immortality, which involves a transformation within our core awareness and Self-identity.

Each Life as a Day for the Soul

The daily movement from waking to dream and deep sleep

reflects the longer movement of our souls from one life and incarnation to another. Deep sleep is a partial death as it were, just as death is a long sleep.

- Waking relates to our sojourn in physical reality, the realm of dense matter and gross form. This relates to the Earth in yogic thought.
- Dream relates to our sojourn in astral reality, the realm of subtle form, thought and energy. This is sometimes called the atmospheric realm or realm of the Moon in yogic thought.
- Deep sleep relates to our sojourn in formless causal realms of seed energy and light. This relates to Heaven, the realm of space or the Sun in yogic thought.[17]

The experience of death and rebirth is much like sleep, dream and reawakening on a daily level. Death is but a prolonged sleep in which we have prolonged dreams, including images of heavens and purgatories, and eventually awaken in a new physical incarnation. The main difference is that while we remember our previous day's activity very well, we seldom remember anything about our past lives. That memory of past lives is also facilitated by crossing over deep sleep.

Each day we undergo a mini birth and death. The self that wakes up is like a rebirth of the self that went to sleep the night before. We relinquish the old every night and take up the new every morning. We usually forget this daily change of who we are, but for those who are continuously aware it is easy to see. The enlightened soul awakens to a new reality and new perception of truth every morning.

In this regard there is an important awareness experiment to explore. Try to hold a certain thought right before you go to sleep at night and then remember it when you first awaken in the morning. It may be a mantra, a prayer, a wish or intention – whatever you like. You may forget what it was at first. Write the thought down and check in the morning to see if it still resonates with you. This thought may be a mantra, an intention or a vision. Over time your ability to link your previous night's awareness with the new morning's awareness will grow. Eventually you will be able to hold a steady focus throughout sleep as well.

If we can master the daily movement from waking to deep sleep, we can also master our greater soul's journey through the physical, astral and causal worlds. If we can live one day fully in consciousness, we can conquer death and transcend time and space. The mysteries of day and night are profound. The universe itself has its longer day and night of universal activity and universal rest extending over many billions of years. Yet each day in time reflects the full cycle of cosmic existence and can allow us to comprehend it as a whole.

Every Day as the Creation of the Entire Universe

The deep sleep state can be identified with *Mula Prakriti* or the root substance of the universe, out of which all forms are fashioned. If we can remain conscious and observe it, we can penetrate to the very origin of creation. We can experience the creation of the universe every day, its unfoldment from pure consciousness to gross materiality, through the cosmic OM vibration and its various levels of expression and densification.

Underlying deep sleep is the consciousness of *Ishvara*, the Creator, Preserver and Transformer of all, with which our soul is ultimately one. We can experience every day how Ishvara creates and absorbs everything in consciousness. This Ishvara is the *Adi Guru* or original teacher of Yoga through the cosmic vibration OM (Pranava) as is taught in the *Yoga Sutras*.[18] Our individual soul mirrors this cosmic creative process within the mind in own daily cycle of consciousness.

In truth all eternity is present at every moment of time. Each day and night of our lives reflects the cosmic movement of time overall as the day and night of Brahman, with day as the cosmic creation and night as its withdrawal or pralaya. Everything in the universe is flashing off and on, manifesting and dissolving, in various interdependent cycles, ultimately like flashes of cosmic lightning.

Eternity is the unending day of pure consciousness, whose dualistic shadows of day and night form our outer world of experience. Once we remove the veil of ignorance from our minds, such perpetual inner light will become a constant experience.

Similarly, at every point in space is the infinite, overflowing with Brahmandas or cosmic eggs, unfolding various world systems in innumerable dimensions. Our personal dream of life is rooted in the universal dream of life that is vast and endless. Through deep meditation we can learn to awaken beyond time and its cycles, yet hold these cycles within us, contemplating the cosmic dream.

Each cycle of time holds the entire movement of time, starting with the days and nights. We must learn to use the movement of time to go beyond time, which is to integrate all time cycles in the still point of pure consciousness within us that is ever awake and aware.

Part III

Practices of the Yoga of Consciousness through the Four States

Awakening from the Cosmic Dream

Our lives are but a long sleep and dream – not of a mere personal nature but of our deeper soul that has had numerous lives in many worlds of experience. Our physical lives are based upon forgetting our eternal origin and falling into the allure of a glittering external reality, in which we lose our true spiritual identity and think of ourselves as only the physical body.

How long does our physical life and consciousness actually endure? Most of us will reply as long as a lifetime of many decades, now usually eighty years or more. However, the fact is that physical awareness is interrupted, if not broken, every day by the state of sleep. We spend around eight hours a day or about a third of our lives in the state of sleep, in which our physical life is put into abeyance.

We are cosmic beings asleep in the dream of physical reality, trapped in an apparent bodily identity in the material world. In our true nature, we are not bodies or even minds but consist of the energy and light of consciousness that is capable of taking innumerable forms in a variety of worlds and different dimensions. We can return to that higher light at any moment and jump beyond time and space, birth and death, if our vision is single and clear, turned within.

We are the spirit, formless and all-pervasive, though confined in an apparent bondage to a dense physical cage. In dream and deep sleep this inner spirit can expand out of its bodily limitations and touch its wider abodes of expression and existence, but we fail to heed these intimations and their profound implications. We focus obsessively on the outer world of the waking state and miss the inner potentials of dream, sleep and beyond.

For any genuine Yoga practice to proceed, we must awaken to our inner Self or soul that is the true being underlying the three states of waking, dream and deep sleep. We must practice Yoga in all the three states, not just in the waking body and mind. This will allow us access to the fourth transcendent state beyond waking and sleep, the state of Self-awareness that is the goal of all Yoga practice.

Yoga as the development of consciousness is performed by the inner Self, not by the outer mind and body. This requires a radical turn within, looking beyond the world. Yet we all sense our eternal reality and Divine home and can awaken to its memory as it abides forever within us.

The Fact of Impermanence

What most characterizes a dream is that what happens in dream is a momentary affair limited to our own minds, with no lasting result that we can verify in the outer world. Once a dream is over, its experience comes to an end and is quickly forgotten, its reality discountenanced. You cannot visit your dream locations in the waking state and share them with others. We can subjectively experience great success or difficulties in the dream state, but cannot take them seriously once we awaken.

Yet though the waking state is more enduring than dream, it has similar temporal limitations. It eventually comes to an end and must be forgotten. Once it is over, a waking experience is finished much like a dream. Over time we are unable to remember actual events in our personal lives apart from dreams and imaginations, which color even our memories. As we contemplate our past experiences, it is hard to discriminate what actually occurred from how it affected us or what we might have wanted it to be.

The waking state is a kind of collective dream that is shared and prolonged. We experience a common waking world that appears fixed in nature, what we call the material world. But if we examine it carefully we see that physical reality is shifting every second and is hardly as stable as it superficially appears to be. Modern physics has deconstructed physical reality and shown it to be an illusion of subtle particles and energy fields in a vast interconnected universe of space and light. This cosmos of relativity in time and space seems very much like the forms and patterns of dreams and fantasies but on a grander scale.

Behind the apparent stability of the material world are constant changes that reveal its illusory nature. The movement of the day from sunrise to sunset shows its transient nature, with morning quickly turning into afternoon and evening. The shift of the seasons is the prime factor of change and transformation in the world of nature. The outer rush of prana in the springtime is followed by its inward withdrawal in the autumn, as with the budding and falling of the leaves.

Yet most important for us is the aging process through our biological clock, showing us that the physical body is not a fixed reality but a limited movement in time. Our ultimate death forms the big question mark behind the reality of the physical world, our bodily self and all of its experiences. While we try to remain oblivious to this fact of death, it remains as the event horizon of our lives that everything else must lead to.

Meanwhile, our minds change much more quickly than our bodies, going through significant ups and downs in the period of a few minutes, sometimes seconds, which can be dramatic or even contradictory. Even our ideas of who we are, what our life means, who our friends are, or what is truth are constantly shifting and caught in duality.

Change is the prime reality and driving energy operating in the material world. Life is a play of dynamic forces, not simply a set of fixed forms or structures. Material stasis is but a short sojourn in a longer movement of transformation from beginning to end, birth to death.

The transience of our lives reveals their dream-like nature. Eventually –however things may appear to last, however much we may seem to gain or to lose – they come to an end, which is to end up as nothing, whether it is yesterday's food, our own childhood experiences, or the public achievements of our adult life. The tragedy of individuals who die young is a reflection of this unpredictable transience of life. In fact, none of us can be guaranteed that this current day is not our last!

Most of us have experienced this truth of impermanence in dramatic ways, for example, going back to old family homes and finding that these have radically changed or that they are no more. We all lose friends and family members in the course of time. Sometimes the world loses interest in us, particularly as we become older. Even if great world leaders pass away, in a few weeks they too are forgotten, except for a few memorials. The movement of time is relentless and leaves nothing and no one standing in the end.

This dramatic experience of impermanence is the basis of great art and literature, particularly tragedies. A sense of possible loss permeates our emotions and relationships. On one level, it helps us better appreciate our transient existence, but mostly we live in a daily denial of the fact that the sands of time are running out on us. We are unhappy facing the fact that we ourselves will eventually die and not know what if anything within us is likely to continue. Yet we conveniently choose not to remember this.

This fact of death, however, can arouse a profound wisdom and a heartfelt aspiration within us. Our longing for eternal existence reflects the deeper reality of our soul, which is not bound by time. To discover that immortal soul we must move beyond the illusion of time created in our physical world. We must stop cherishing the transient, become detached from it, and search for what is truly eternal, of which the transient is at best an intimation.

Our transient physical life is but the creative imagination of our immortal soul. In the darkness of deep sleep we forget our cosmic reality and fall into a limited outward looking awareness. This stupor of the ego state causes us to take the physical body as our true nature and forget the unlimited wellsprings of consciousness within us. The obscuring power of deep sleep remains in the background throughout waking and dream, veiling us from our deeper reality. It is out of the darkness of deep sleep that our dreams arise and our waking consciousness is limited and distorted.

The Variability of our Waking Life

Our waking material world does not present us with lasting certainties but only with shifting phenomena. There is a tremendous variability to our world and our experience of it. It is very hard to accurately judge any person or event because of these variabilities, however physically real the appearance may be.

We can start with the simple variabilities of the weather, which changes regularly and often in an unpredictable or sudden manner. Then there are variabilities in our own moods. We may meet someone on a day in which we are feeling unwell and they may judge us to be aloof and hard to communicate with, not knowing our internal condition. The entire world is a variable phenomenon, not a fixed reality. We see glimpses and sides of things but not the whole or the essence.

This variability of experience means that we are always dealing with probabilities, not things that must happen. We are rarely certain what will be or when, though we can usually surmise what will likely occur within workable parameters. In looking to the future we can only postulate trends and possibilities. Yet even in the present moment most of what we are working with are only probabilities. We try to shape forces in the present to yield the results we would like to occur over time, not being certain of the actual eventual results. Our life is malleable, more like a wave on the sea than a rock in the ground. We cannot even be certain what our own children will end up becoming.

The "uncertainty principle", such as we find in modern physics, is inherent in our waking lives. This may lead to insecurity, as life has its share of sorrow, or it may cause us to be happy with the unpredictability and ever newness of life. We only know what things appear to be, are likely to be or may eventually become at a certain point of time and space. There are many rainbows, shadows and mirages both within and around us.

In addition, each one of us is not a homogeneous or fully integrated being. We are composite creatures – a combination of physical, psychological, social and spiritual forces, with different layers and aspects, and many internal contradictions owing to the diverse energies at work within us. We possess hidden strengths and weaknesses, higher capacities and lower impulses that may emerge at any given point of time. Which of those dominate in the end depends upon our degree of awareness and how we can harmonize the interaction of this transient array of forces that compose us.

A certain unpredictable chemistry happens in life. For example, chemical compounds that are harmless in themselves can be used to make bombs by adding other chemicals to them, like explosives made with certain types of otherwise harmless fertilizers. Similarly combinations of people, experiences, times or places can end up producing powerful positive or negative results, very different from what the individual factors involved might have indicated.

The Illusion of Waking Reality

Our primary reality as long as we are alive is the waking world. Most of us take this waking reality to be our true existence, however painful, uncertain, unfulfilling or temporary it may be. For all practical purposes it is our home, identity, and place of action. We regard dream and deep sleep as interludes, mere biological periods of rest, during the longer movement of our waking lives, although they are actually indications of its limitations.

We seek happiness, knowledge and fulfillment in the world of our waking experience through its physical vehicle. This partial vision blinds us to the greater reality and the depths of consciousness beyond this earthly realm. We must learn to acknowledge the soul's call to awaken to our eternal abode in the pure light of awareness.

Our waking mind develops knowledge of the external world, but however much we learn, there is much more that remains unknown to us. All the databases and facts that modern information technology has gathered, fail to explain the basic mystery of life and consciousness that is beyond all calculation.

We have sufficient experience of the transience and uncertainty of waking life to make us question its reality – and instead question whether sleep, dream and higher states of consciousness may reflect a greater reality. But we seldom seriously consider what our daily experience is teaching us about its limitations. Though we continuously lose things or forget them, we are more concerned with the new things we might yet acquire, though we will not be able to hold on to these either. Each day we must make great efforts to sustain the continuity of our lives with new adjustments to ever changing circumstances.

Differences in Waking Reality

Our waking life is not a uniform experience for everyone. Different individuals, societies and cultures experience waking life differently and have divergent ideas of reality or the meaning of life. Such ideas and experiences have also varied considerably throughout history.

Many traditional cultures afford a greater importance to the dream state and realities beyond the physical, honoring all life as sacred and finding the spirit to exist everywhere. Australian aborigines live in dreamtime. Medieval western religious cultures looked more to heaven than to earthly life as their ultimate abode.

Our modern society seems to be the most physically oriented of all cultures, which we call being rational and scientific. This means that we dismiss realities beyond the material world as illogical, lacking in evidence or as the product of superstition. Such views show a limited vision, particularly as science continues to deconstruct the reality of the external world and the ego self.

Our waking life appears to be objective as it is held in common with other people. Growing up we learn how to function in the material world and establish a place and home within it. This begins with gaining control of our biological functions when children, extending to education, work and family life as we age. Most of us are successful in functioning in the material world until we get too old or ill to do so, which confronts us with the illusory nature of physical reality. We know that the world endures even if we die. Yet if we look closely we see that the world itself as a process in time is subject to similar periods of decline and termination as we are, with everyone who is born also eventually dying. Changes in the social order can also be dramatic or unexpected as history and even current politics so often reveal.

We experience many disruptions in our physical reality, with disease and sorrow at a personal level. There are wars, crimes and social problems at a collective level, and with natural calamities in the world of nature. Our physical reality however apparently solid is not at all a certain, safe or secure place, but requires constant attention and caution to maintain, with inevitable dangers regularly along the way.

Our waking self is also a dream entity, a kind of puppet pulled by outside forces, a hypnosis to the external world that can only be broken by the insight born of deep meditation. *Maya or the world as illusion in Vedic thought reflects the condition of being trapped in the waking state as real.* Moving out of Maya is aided by gaining greater awareness in dream and deep sleep, from which Maya arises.

Mind as a Subconscious Process

The human mind is not a true conscious intelligence but only a half-waking, half-sleeping awareness. We can observe this fact in the amount of time we spend in the states of dream and deep sleep. Yet even during waking hours, we frequently get lost in routines in which the mind works mechanically. Other times we are caught in own fantasies and daydreams and slip out of waking attention, which we find to be too much work to steadily maintain.

Much of our waking state consists of half-dreaming wandering mind, scattered thoughts, disturbed emotions, or random sensations. We are often caught up in meaningless distractions or trivial pursuits. Gossip and worry often dominate our waking hours; though they may have little to do with what actually is happening to us personally.

Our emotions are also half-aware states – subconscious states in which emotional forces take over minds and distort our rational faculties. Our numerous emotions extend from fear, anger, desire and envy to every sort of wishful thinking, bordering on neurosis and psychosis. When we are caught in an emotion, which is common almost every day, like when we are taken over by anger, we are almost in a dream state. Our perception and judgment is clouded by the emotion, to the extent that we may needlessly harm not only other people but also ourselves.

Enjoyment through the senses is another half-aware state. We get caught in momentary enjoyments and forget the rest of life and the world of nature, much as we do in the dream state. We observe this while people are eating something tasty, for example, becoming unaware of the world around them in the process, but it extends to all sensory enjoyments. In spite of the fact that we think the material world is real, we seem happiest when we are able to forget the greater world in the fascination of some particular enjoyment or addictive sensation.

Mass entertainment modern media form of enjoyment is

another kind of semi-dream state in which we allow external sensations to drive our minds. We observe this when we are watching an engrossing movie. The movie is like a dream we are experiencing that has little to do with us personally and may not reflect any actual events, yet can engage us much more than our own activity. We seek leisure in such entertainment-based distractions that are more imagination than anything real.

We have a deep-seated need and craving for dreamlike fantasy experiences even in the waking state, which also tells us its dreamlike nature. If we can cultivate the power of dreamlike imagination consciously, it can create wonderful works of art and serve a great purpose in life inspiring us to dream, evolve and transcend. Such creative fantasy is not simply negative or misleading but suggests to us that the world in which we live is ultimately but a creation of our own thoughts with much more hidden than we are currently manifesting.

Calculation, perhaps surprisingly to some, is another state of half-awareness and can be dreamlike in nature. Calculations are habitual and can become obsessions that we repeat without thinking. We get immersed in statistics, numbers and formulas and lose our actual awareness of the world around us. We give more importance to numbers than to the actualities of life. We regard our measurements of the world as more important than the world itself.

We clearly observe this dream like quality of the number based mind in pursuit of sports statistics that we carefully memorize and think about, though it has little to do with our own lives. Such calculation obsessions are now allied with fantasy games in which we can lose ourselves altogether in media images. Games overall have a semi-dream like or fantasy quality, in which we forget our physical reality and take on new identities or proxies, or identify with heroes. We are happy when our team wins and distressed when it loses, even though its gain or loss has little to do with us.

We see this same fantasy and speculation model in an obsession with stock markets, in which we often imagine great gains for ourselves. Calculation[19] gets us caught in the waves of outer experience, immersing us in the measurements and divisions of Maya, which means that which is measured. For us the measurement becomes more important or real than what it measures, just as the name often becomes more important than the actual person it is associated with.

Addictions are perhaps the most significant indication that our waking life is not fully aware or even in our control. Most of us have various addictions, many apparently harmless like sugar or coffee, others dangerous like opiates. These extend to behavioral addictions like sex addictions or even workaholics. Addictions and difficulty in overcoming them are a good indication that our waking state is not fully awake and that we are not in control of our own minds.

The mind itself is inherently a kind of addiction creating mechanism, reflecting memory patterns, habit, impulse and conditioning; and not conscious choice and perception. The mind seeks the comfort and security of repetition and likes to keep us in a semi-awake state of habitual activity. It prefers to be habituated to something, particularly powerful sensations of pleasure, even pain. This inertia of the mind is a kind of sleep or state of dullness and limited awareness. It projects dreams, fantasies, speculations, emotions or misperceptions as reality. In the minds' conditioned actions, we fail to be truly aware, to know ourselves, or know the nature of reality. To wake up to reality, we must wake up from all the fantasies, fears and desires of the mind, or we will remain spiritually asleep as long as we live. This requires moving beyond the mind to a higher consciousness, not clouded by its conditioning.

The Outer Nature of the Mind

Your mind does not belong to you. The mind and its conditioning are actually external to your consciousness that is ever free. The mind is part of nature or Prakriti and belongs to the external world, not to your inner being (the Purusha of yogic thought). The mind is not a form of true Self-awareness. The mind is a communication and action device necessary for expression and interaction in the outer world. The mind is relational in nature. Your mind also belongs to your family, friends, society, language and education.

Your thoughts reflect your social interactions perhaps more so than anything else and is more collective than individual. Our minds are made up of the opinions of other people that we have imbibed over time and reflect little original thinking of our own. Like people in a room, these opinions contest for our attention at the level of thought and memory. When we try to make up our minds we are usually trying to figure out what internalized voice of other people to listen to and follow as if it were own.

Our minds are connected to the society we are part of and reflect its values, customs and compulsions. This social part of the mind reflects the different individuals and groups we are connected to, not only at the level of attraction but also at the level of repulsion. Our behavior is rooted in countering the people we do not like, perhaps more so than following those that we do. Each mind contains many people and has many voices, which are often in conflict and are rarely under the command of the conscious self.

The mind is like a ghost or shadow, a residue of external

interactions, reflecting their entropy and influence over us. This begins with a socially based education that passes on collective memories to us as if they were our own, the glory of our country, community or religion, for examples. The mind has no essence of its own. It reflects the light of awareness from our inner consciousness, but distorts it through its own karmic patterns, fears and desires.

Part of the mind reflects the physical body and its biological needs. Yet the more we focus on the physical body as our true identity, the more unconscious we tend to become. The body itself as a formation of dense matter has a tamasic or inertia based nature that draws our awareness into physical habits and compulsion.

The physical world is dominated by material and unconscious forces and patterns. The more we look outward, the more unaware we become. The mind as conditioned to the body and material world possesses an inherent entropy towards limited awareness that blocks an ability to connect to the deeper consciousness within us.

The Phantasmagoria of the Senses

Our physical world consists of a complex set of impressions, a phantasmagoria put together by the senses as interpreted by the mind.

- The sense of sight provides us with our main image or idea of the world overall, its forms, distances and dimensions.
- Sound provides us main means of communication with others and interaction with the world.
- Touch, taste and smell provide us more physically-based

sensations, enjoyments and bodily connections, affording us a sense of our own physical reality.

The senses do not allow us to perceive the true nature of things, but only provide an outer and partial view that is of temporary value. The limitations of our sensory acuity are well known to all of us, whether it is the limited range of our vision and hearing, or their deterioration with age or injury.

Sensory impressions are always limited, one-sided and superficial. They do not reveal the enduring inner essence or reality but only an appearance at a particular point of time and space that may quickly change. The senses hide as much as they reveal.

Sensory images, which require interpretation by the mind, are merely suggestive, not final. Sensations stimulate memory and imagination, causing us to project fantasies of what we would like to happen or to achieve. For example, the sight of a beautiful woman affects the male senses differently than the female senses. Or the smell of food to a hungry person is more powerful than to one who has just eaten. The biological imperatives inherent in the senses compel us to act, rather than merely provide accurate information about the external world. The senses have many inherent biases, most of which we have experienced but have seldom adequately examined.

We spend much time trying to determine the reality of things behind their appearances, whether it is what we are seeking to buy, our relationships, or who we truly are inside ourselves. We struggle to discover what is behind the curtain, package, veil or clothing. The development of inner intelligence requires learning to discriminate between how things appear and what they actually are, the two possibly being radically different. Vedic thought teaches us that the entire universe is but a reflection within us, like images seen in a mirror—the mirror being our own consciousness.

Indeed sensory perception is as much a type of dreaming as it is a type of direct cognition. Our senses are as much faculties of desire and imagination as a means of objectively determining the nature of any enduring reality. They reflect short-term creaturely needs more so than any lasting truth.

There is a famous old Indian story of five blind men and an elephant, each man coming to a different conclusion about the nature of the elephant, owing to their limited contact with it – one feeling the tusk, one the tail, one the trunk, one the belly and one the leg – each thinking the limited part represented the animal as a whole and each feeling validated about their knowledge with the fact of their experience. The five senses provide us information about the world but it is limited and can obscure or confuse us as much as it can bring clarity. We must strive to understand who we truly are as conscious perceivers behind the sensory illusion of the physical body and its constant changes, or the mind's shifting moods and opinions.

Today in the information entertainment era many people are living more in fantasy than in any clear waking consciousness. We have invested our lives with a virtual reality including social media images and biodatas that we project as who we really are. We live not merely in a body but in front of a screen on which we project fantasy lives. Yet while technology shows us how to expand and manipulate physical reality, we seldom use it to take the next step. Were we to use technology to question physical reality we may be surprised to discover it to be only a media-like concoction brewed by our own mind and senses.

The Illusion of Waking Time

We are constantly moving in and out of time – the word "time" referring to the "present moment". We are perpetually checking in and out of the waking world, with the mind alternating its attention between the waking world and fantasy or imagined reality elsewhere, extending into the remembered past and the imagined future.

The continuity of chronological time in the waking state is an illusion. We are not equally aware at every moment, nor is our awareness of chronological time continuous. In some instances we find time to be moving too slowly, like when we are waiting in a long line of people. At other instances we find time moving too quickly like when we are really enjoying ourselves. We have our own biological and psychological time sense in the waking state with its own rhythms, its own continuity and yet discontinuity, colored by both outer events and inner feelings; a time sense that is different for each one of us.

While we live in the waking world, we often find waking activity to be insufficient, boring, tedious or painful. To escape that boredom, we daydream, follow entertainment or listen to the news, distracting ourselves in one way or another. We are not always comfortable with the waking reality and find it to be a temporary construction we would like to change. If we are unable to actually change our material lives, we may imagine or speculate on something better, to the extent of imagining that we have a different partner or that we ourselves are a different person.

The Illusions of the Media

The waking world that we observe through the mass media is very much a filtered phenomena that can have little resemblance to the reality of our personal lives. The media presents us with a view of the world designed to further its own commercial, political and cultural vested interests. *The media is the Maya of the Maya, taking illusory appearances to a more limited, though more exotic level of illusion.* We replace the vastness of our sensory perception of nature with a focus on a small box or entertainment screen where time is controlled and events are scaled down and interpreted for us, often with the intention to program our behavior in one direction or another.

This means that during our waking state, we are actually wakeful, aware and attentive only part of the time, if at all. The waking mind is a conditioned half-conscious intelligence, struggling to be aware, but not of objective awareness itself. Instead, it is often working out of impulses born of ignorance, like wanting to be more aware to gain the dream commodities of physical reality, such as more pleasure, money or power.

Our minds easily fall into subconscious states in which our waking awareness gets clouded and confused. The waking mind is not a wakeful clear intelligence, but distorted by memory and imagination. Its perception is conditioned and often contrived, seeing what we want to see rather than what is actually there. The mind is not self-aware but is the product of impulses it does not understand, impulses originated in dream and sleep.

Waking reality is a long drawn out illusion of the waking mind. Whatever we may see objectively is colored and placed in its context by the mind, in which true reality is obscured by the biases and compulsions of the mind. This consists of not only misinterpreting the feelings of others, but also misinterpreting the world of nature. We may see something through the senses but we do not know what is actually there over time or what its true reality is.

The Inherent Ignorance and Sleep behind the Waking State

Ignorance and unconsciousness is the very nature of physical reality that we contact in the waking state. Limited knowledge of the mind and senses, and the density of physical matter, extending to the dullness of our own bodies indicates this state of wrong perception. This ignorance is a kind of sleep, and reflects the sleep of the soul, which is held in the state of deep sleep.

Ignorance is twofold as both natural and karmic.

- Our natural ignorance is rooted in biological compulsions that cause us to regard as real what upholds our biological needs, like hunger and thirst that drive us to fulfill them before anything else.

  This means that we may not be interested in knowledge of a higher nature if we have not dealt with the necessities of our outer lives or if such knowledge is not relevant to them.

- Karmic ignorance is what arises from our individual actions, the values that we have and the goals that we are seeking. Our karma sculpts a kind of reality but it is based upon the inertia of our desires and the wishful thinking behind them.

  This means that we may not want to know the truth. We prefer what is pleasant or what caters to our desires, and will avoid or discountenance what is unpleasant or goes against our wishes. As the higher truth does not conform to our desires, we may prefer not to know it.

Overcoming both natural and karmic ignorance is very difficult and requires extensive study and practice, extending to many lifetimes. It is only possible by relentless self-examination.

The true way of human evolution is to awaken from the dream of individual life to discover the cosmic purpose and reality underlying it, to awaken from the dream of transient life to the reality of eternal existence. This is the transformation that is the basis and goal of movement in consciousness that reveals who we truly are. We can only awaken when we first realize the extent and depth to which we are asleep. The entire world is part of a greater sleep and dream.

The Yoga of the Waking State

We perform our yoga practices during the waking state that we regard as our true reality. It focuses on the physical body that we consider to be our true identity. We practice Yoga to make ourselves happier, healthier and more fit to function in the material world. Yoga teachers explain in detail the effects of Yoga on the physical body, its bones, joints, organs and systems, and how it makes the body function better, with greater vitality and immunity, making us feel better overall. While that is a good place to start, it is but the first step into the wider universe of Yoga. The goal of Yoga is to detach us from the body and take us beyond all time and space.

Similarly, we practice meditation to improve mental focus and performance in the waking state, so that we can counter stress and perform better in our work, relationships or studies. Science examines the effects of meditation on brain chemistry and brain waves, how it harmonizes the nervous and endocrine systems – judging meditation by its results in enhancing our bodily experience of life, as if the physical brain were the true seat of awareness and the measure of intelligence. Again that is a good place to start, but it is a very diminished view of meditation, which is meant to take us beyond both body and mind.

In Yoga and meditation practices, we seldom question the validity of the waking state and the reality of the material world revealed through the body and senses. We rarely consider the need to discover our deeper nature and eternal reality, though this has always been the stated purpose of traditional Yoga. The Yoga of the Waking State connects our daily Yoga practice with the higher wakefulness that allows us to awaken to our true Self in all that we do.

Yoga from its origins aims at the development of higher consciousness, leading us to Self-realization, through the cultivation of "samadhi" or unity consciousness, which requires moving beyond the normal dualistic perceptions of our waking reality. To truly practice Yoga we must learn to transcend the waking state and physical reality into the deeper awareness within us that cannot be limited to time, place or person.

Reaching a true yogic consciousness requires deconstructing our sense of physical reality, which is a product of limited awareness. This means moving beyond any sense of bodily identity and any restriction to time-space reality as defining our existence. Without taking our awareness beyond the worldly self, we are not truly practicing meditation or Yoga in the true sense of these terms, but just enhancing our illusions.

Deconstructing physical reality means removing our identification with body, senses, prana and mind. It requires us to cease taking outer appearances as real and instead see them as manifestations of a deeper light of consciousness with no separate reality of their own. This is certainly a daunting task and one that few of us may be willing to attempt, but is necessary if we truly aspire to go beyond death and sorrow.

Yet if we look closely at modern physics and the new information technology, we can observe a similar deconstruction of physical reality in favor of a universe of energy and information, not fixed material forms, with each individual connected to the entire cosmos. The yogic deconstruction of physical reality may just be mirroring the future humanity as we extend our sense of reality beyond personal and bodily limitations.

Defining the Yoga of the Waking State

The Yoga of the Waking State can simply be defined as the Yoga of conscious wakefulness. The practice of becoming more consciously aware in the waking state is the Yoga of the Waking State.

We must learn to use the waking state to awaken yet more deeply to our inner reality, not just to the outer realm of the senses. We must reclaim our true nature as pure consciousness, the eternal witness of all phenomena. We must abide in an ever-deepening vibrant wakeful awareness, and not just experience the waking state of the physical body. We must awaken to our inner being and Cosmic Self.

Yoga as a process of developing an inner awareness encourages us to abide in a state of permanent wakefulness. A clear observant wakeful awareness should be our priority, attaining it within a short meditation practice to start with, but eventually retaining it throughout the day. The Yoga of the waking state also requires bringing a waking awareness into dream and deep sleep, and finally becoming a Yoga of all the four states that takes us to the transcendent, which is a state of an eternally wakeful existence beyond time and space, body and mind.

There is a special yogic potential for higher awareness hidden in the waking state that we must appreciate and cultivate. It is an ability to hold to a clear and direct perception of what things are, to recognize what is. Such a clear waking awareness allows us to become observant, noting more and more what is actually transpiring within and around us – not only colorful appearances and dramatic events but subtle nuances, extending into space, silence and solitude. It means giving up the desires and fantasies of the waking mind and developing a greater detachment from the body; thus becoming an observer not weighed down by any biases or opinions.

The movement of deep meditation inherently involves cultivating an ongoing state of wakefulness, aiming to become fully conscious and attentive in all that we think or do. The waking state should be a cultivation of the Yoga of wakefulness and direct perception, in which we discern the true essence of awareness from the manifests of outer names and forms in the material world. It should be a growth in contemplative inspiration and not just a confinement within our thoughts and fantasies.

Yet much of the time during the day we are half asleep, falling into speculation, imagination, daydreams, habits and enjoyment, which results in an overall loss of self-awareness. We are seldom present in a state of true wakeful awareness even while technically awake. That the body is awake does not necessarily mean that our minds are awake. And that our minds are awake does not necessarily mean that our inner consciousness is awake. Usually, it is just the opposite. Body and mind are forms of limited consciousness, compulsion and conditioning. Being awake in body and mind does not awaken our inner awareness without special practices designed to do so.

We are kept awake externally by the distractions of the senses. This is a state of wakefulness brought about by outer stimulation and not by the true inner creative intelligence. Once this sensory noise shuts down we easily fall into dullness or sleep, having no creative wellspring of consciousness within us to motivate our own original thoughts and actions to motivate us.

In the new modern media era, an ever more diverse pursuit of entertainment dominates our waking lives, through which we lose the inner light of awareness to the commercial world. We confuse gathering of media information as an aid to being aware. In addition to outer sensory experience, we treat media screens as essential to our waking lives, forgetting the inner awareness that inherently transcends these outer manifestations.

True wakefulness consists of remaining mindfully aware at every moment, observing the world without choice or expectations, rather than pursuing it with desire and ambition. This wakeful awareness has its own beauty and bliss that does not rely on anything on the outside for its happiness. There is nothing that the external world can offer you, no matter how extraordinary, that can compare to the magic of awareness, perception and insight within you. This does not mean you should not be cognizant of what is happening in the outer world. Instead you should place such events, however practically important, in the context of a deeper vision of the transcendent.

We all have moments of clarity in the waking state that we value but we do not know how to develop or prolong them into a continual awareness. These clear moments allow us to make right decisions and guide our lives with wisdom. But few of us consciously cultivate the state of wakeful awareness or are taught how to do so. The result is that our waking clarity does not grow or reach its full potential.

It may sound odd but *we need to cultivate staying awake while we are physically awake*, rather than drifting off into mechanical or compulsive reactions, and getting lost in the dream of the material world. Emotions are largely subconscious reactions, rather than conscious responses. Fear, anger and desire are reactive impulses, not intelligent ways to interact with the world. If we examine our so-called waking state, we will find that there is little true wakefulness within it. Instead it has predominantly distracted or dull states of mind (rajasic and tamasic states according to the language of Yoga).

The Yoga of the waking state requires cultivating moment-by-moment wakefulness. All its potential techniques and practices are supports for this greater endeavor. There are many ways to help us become more aware while in our waking lives. If we can follow these out, we can carry them into dream, sleep and beyond.

Wakeful awareness, we should note, is not limited to the waking state or to the activity of the human brain, but is the nature of pure consciousness underlying all the movements of the mind. Cultivating wakefulness is a way to go beyond all the cycles of time. It is not simply a means of being aware in the present moment. It is a way of stepping out of time itself, be it past, present or future. All true learning consists of awakening to our eternal nature that is hidden underneath all that we do and are.

True wakefulness consists of being awake in our inner being as the Self of all, not simply being temporarily cognizant of the shifting phenomena of the waking state. Inner wakefulness requires that we recognize the material world as a karmic dream and the physical body as only its dream vehicle and not our true nature. We must awaken from the dream of spiritual ignorance in which we have forgotten our immortal nature and life purpose. There are many ways to develop this Yoga of the waking state or waking awareness, from conscious action to silent meditation.

The Yoga of Clear Perception

The essence of waking consciousness consists of clear perception, not clouded by dullness or fantasy, sleep or dream.

To cultivate this state of clarity as a Yoga practice, we must strive to be wakefully aware at all times and in all places, and never be caught in distraction, routine or habit. This means to be aware of the movement of life and its transformations at a subtle level at every instant, particularly in the world of nature.

Central to the Yoga of the Waking State is developing an inner state of seeing that extends beyond the physical senses – a seeing that is not clouded by the conditioning and compulsions of the mind. We must recognize our true nature as the Seer, and seeing as the essence of our being, not simply as a function of body or mind – the Seer that is the Purusha or the goal of Yoga practice.[20] True waking consciousness is connected to our deeper Self-awareness. It is not a product of the physical body or brain. Wakefulness is the true nature of consciousness beyond its identification with body and mind that draw it into ignorance and distraction.

This wakeful state of Yoga must not be confused with the ordinary sense of merely feeling awake. It is a heightened wakeful state in which the mind is held in a state of detached perception and observation, not agitated by emotion, sensation or opinion. It is a discerning wakeful attention very different from an entranced involvement in sensory activity. Such true wakefulness requires observing physical and mental states with rigorous discernment and detachment, never getting carried away by them even for an instant.

A related aspect of the Yoga of the Waking state is to merge into objective reality or Pure Existence (the Brahman of Vedantic thought). This means to not mistake material objects as real in themselves. One should first perceive the presence of being and the light that prevails vividly in the waking state, and from this state observe the objects around us with clarity and detachment. It is to become a mirror for all that we see and experience in life.

To be aware of things as they are is to recognize them like clouds in the sky or waves on the sea – not as real in themselves but as manifestations of a higher light and energy of consciousness.

Asana and Awareness of the Physical Body

All Yoga practices can be used to develop wakeful awareness, which is the foundation of Yoga, starting with Yoga asanas, which require wakeful attention for their proper performance. When we become truly aware of our body as an instrument of an expression, rather than as our true identity, we naturally become detached from it. The body becomes an object of observation for a deeper consciousness. We gradually realize that we are not the body, which is a formation of various tissues and organs that are constantly changing. We gradually realize that we are the being and energy operating the body. Physical stillness through asana allows us to let go of body consciousness as it puts the body to rest.

Unfortunately, many people today mistake "awareness of the body" to mean developing more body consciousness; and focus on how we look, how others see us, or how attractive or fit we appear. This is not true awareness of the body but only an increased bodily attachment. We must not confuse such trying to look good at a physical level with any higher awareness. It actually pulls our consciousness down. You are not your bodily image but the awareness that came into the body at birth and will leave it at death.

To develop a greater awareness relative to the body, we should cultivate the following thoughts and attitudes:

> *"I am the inner power that moves the body, I am not the body itself."*
>
> *"I am not made up of organs or tissues. These are of the body alone, which is my instrument."*
>
> *"I do not have arms and legs; it is the body which has arms and legs. My form is pure consciousness."*
>
> *"The body moves; I do not move. My awareness is ever present through every movement of the body as its guiding light and directing energy."*

Such self-examination procedures in asana practice can help us develop a higher awareness and wakefulness overall. But if we worry about how we look during the practice, then such asana practice will keep us trapped in physical reality. It will not develop any true freedom within us.

Whenever you perform an asana, hold the thought: "I am performing this asana with my outer physical vehicle. May my inner awareness flow throughout and permeate my body with a higher consciousness not bound by bodily pleasure or pain."

Remember that the siddhi or goal of asana practice is to be able to sit silently in meditation, forgetting the body and relaxing into the Infinite.

Pranayama as Awareness of the Breath

Our prana is active outwardly in the waking state, easily distracted and involved in the external world through the senses. If we learn to turn our prana within through pranayama and awareness of the breath then our prana can become a force for a deeper wakefulness.

When we become aware of the breath at an inner level, we naturally become detached from it. Breathing consciously is the beginning of awareness of the breath. Awareness of the breath is the beginning of awareness of prana. We should ultimately be aware that our entire life is a manifestation of an inner consciousness in its journey to Self-realization.

To develop this greater awareness of the breath, we should cultivate the following thoughts and attitudes:

> *"I am the one who breathes; I am not the breath."*

> *"The lungs breathe; I do not breathe. My awareness is continuous throughout every breath."*

> *"I have never taken any breath and do not depend upon the breath of the body for my survival. I am the immortal pranic energy underlying body and mind."*

Such aware-breathing naturally develops the inner power of consciousness. It has a great healing and energizing effect as well. It unites and balances all our pranas of body and mind. That conscious prana can be directed anywhere we need to create harmony and balance. This meditation on the breath can be performed with pranic mantras like Hamsa or So'ham, the natural sounds of the breath. Withdrawing our pranic fixation from the body liberates the spirit.

Pratyahara and Awareness of the Senses

Pratyahara or yogic control of the senses has many methods but the prime approach is to cultivate a detached awareness of the senses and their actions. When we become consciously aware of our senses, we naturally become detached from their actions. The senses take on a contemplative function as instruments of an inner knowing, not as mere tools of outer enjoyment. We begin to look for subtle artistic sensations and the hidden presence of peace and bliss (ananda), not just for gross pleasures.

Pratyahara is probably easiest developed through the eyes. To develop a greater awareness of the senses, we should cultivate the following thoughts and attitudes:

> *"I am the one who sees, hears, touches, taste and smells. I am not the sense organs or what they reveal."*
>
> *"My inner light continues throughout all outer manifests experienced through the senses, and continues even when the senses are closed or put to rest."*
>
> *"I am the detached seer of all the movements of body, senses and mind."*

You are the inner seer or light of awareness of which the five senses are mere outer diversifications, like a light filtered through a spectroscope. In all your senses you are simply experiencing different aspects of your own light of consciousness reflected by the external world. You contain all that you see, but integrated into a higher awareness and bliss.

Observing the Mind

Yoga rests upon control of the mind. Yet this has been very much misunderstood. Most efforts to control the mind only serve to disturb it further. True control or calming of the mind arises not through personal effort, which is an action of the mind itself, but through observing our thoughts – the natural control that arises through consciousness, the controller of all. Such higher control of the mind requires detachment from the mind, not fixation on its activities.

Most of the time we are not truly aware of our thoughts but are under their influence, like hypnosis. We are not observing the mind but following the mind's disturbances as if they were our own. Through the mind we get lost in the aspects of the external world that the mind directs us to. To truly observe our thoughts is to introduce space and silence into the mind and become gradually free of thought, replacing a thought dominated state of mind with a contemplative mode.

We need to cultivate a wakeful mind and avoid daydreaming, dullness and inertia. This requires cultivating detachment and letting go of emotions as they arise during the day. We should approach each moment as an inner awakening to a greater truth and reality, and the thoughts of the moment as just surface waves.

To learn how to yogically control the mind and its thoughts, we should cultivate the following thoughts and attitudes:

> *"I am not my thoughts. It is the mind that thinks, not me. I remain the same, present and aware through all the changing thoughts of the mind, which is but my instrument of expression."*

> *"I am the mind behind the mind, the inner knower, pure consciousness and light that is Self-existence, beyond all ideas, concepts and imaginations."*

> *"I am aware without a mind, alive without a body, in my own nature as pure awareness, through which alone the body and mind function."*

When we learn to observe the mind it gradually disappears into the space of awareness. Our thoughts become like clouds in the sky, with nothing to hold on to or possess. Stop being a slave or victim of your thoughts, which are, but vibrations in your mind. Be free of the mind, let go of the past, and be as you are in your true nature.

Observing the Ego

To move beyond the limited self or ego to the true Self or Purusha, we must learn to observe the ego, which is to recognize the limitations of any self-image, bodily identity and its compulsions. The ego after all is rooted in the "I am the body" idea.

At the inmost level, we must learn to observe the ego from a state of detached awareness. This means not falling under the influence of fear or desire, flattery or insult, good fortune or misfortune, pleasure or pain. Whatever anyone may say or think about you, good or bad, has nothing to do with you in your true nature, and merely relates to the body or mind that are not your true Self. You may examine how relevant it is to your outer expressions but should never let it affect your inner awareness.

To transcend the ego and our sense of outer identity, we should cultivate the following thoughts and attitudes:

> *" I have no body and no mind, no self-image, no personal gain or loss. Body and mind are but my instruments of outer expression, not who I really am."*
>
> *"I have no identity in the outer world. My identity is within."*
>
> *"I am pure Self-awareness beyond all objectivity, content in my own nature."*

Let the ego-based self-image dissolve into the light of Self-awareness in which there is no separate self and no other. Return to the state of seeing and no longer regard yourself as an object in the material world. You are the witness of all. Your true Self is nothing in the waking state but is the wakeful witness of all states of mind.

Surrender of the Waking Self

To become truly awake and aware, we must let go of the bodily self of the waking state and realize that it is at best one facet of our greater manifestation in consciousness. The waking ego is but an appearance, a physical construction, and a social role that is always changing. It may have some practical or utilitarian value but is not our essential, enduring or eternal nature. It comes and goes with the movement of time and undergoes momentary fluctuations with all that we do.

Letting go of the waking ego, which is the bodily ego or the "I am the body" idea, creates an inner relaxation and natural expansion of awareness. It means surrendering to the presence of consciousness, in which we offer our self-image as a mere shadow of its light.

The physical body is something that you see and work with but it is not what you are. It is your vehicle for this transient physical life, not the eternal essence of your being. Be kind to your body but do not limit yourself to any bodily identity. You are all pervasive as the light of consciousness. The body is a temple for your inner being, which is the true divinity. Honor your body for what dwells within it, not for its outer appearance.

Self-remembrance

One of the most important practices of true wakefulness is Self-remembrance – remembering our true nature as pure consciousness apart from all the outer phenomena, appearances and actions that we are normally involved with.

True Self-remembrance, we should note, does not consist of merely remembering our personal past or background since birth, which are better forgotten. It requires stepping out of our involvement with time to return to the state of the timeless witness and seer within. If we always remember our inner nature as pure consciousness in whatever we do, we will not lose our attention or identity to the external world. While this practice is useful in all the three states, its importance begins in the waking state itself.

True awakening is to remember our true nature, which requires waking from the cosmic dream while living in physical reality. We must learn to be wakefully aware, using every event or experience in life to wake up further to our inner being. To awaken to the true Self is to move beyond the mind to the Knower within.

Never forget your true Self and you will always remain awake and aware. At the same time, if you fall into dullness or distraction, always remember your true Self beyond all agitation.

General Practices for the Yoga of the Waking State

Below is a summary of the key practices that bring an inner Yoga into the waking state.

- Yoga of OM, chanting and meditating upon OM throughout the day is a helpful support practice to the Yogas of all the Four States.
  Chanting OM first thing in the morning and last thing at night will help us hold wakeful awareness throughout the day and carry it into dream and sleep as well. OM is the mantra of cosmic wakefulness.

- Cultivating the attitude of the witness.
  This is the key practice of yogic meditation, not losing ourselves to the external world, but remaining composed within as we engage with the outer world, as if we were watching a movie and not involved with it. The true witness is always awake. You are the eternal witness of all, including waking and sleep, birth and death.

- Clear awareness and pure perception.
  Reflecting things as they are rather than imposing our opinions and judgments upon them, being above likes and dislikes, love and hate. This also requires letting

other people be who they are and stopping trying to control or manipulate the world around us.

- Surrender of the mind to the inner consciousness that is beyond all compulsions and duality.
  Learning to let go of the mind, that is a state of tension, for effortless awareness that is inner peace. We must always be willing to step beyond the mind, which is but an instrument of thought and expression.

- Self-remembrance.
  Remembering ourselves as the substratum of the waking state, with dream, deep sleep, and cosmic consciousness as deeper aspects of our nature. Awakening to our true Self that is not limited to the cycle of birth and death.

Specific to the Waking State

Below is a summary of the main practices to transform the waking state into yogic meditation.

- Mantra – holding to a mantra throughout the day to remind us of our deeper awareness, like OM Namah Shiva or any special powerful bija mantras you may have been given (like HREEM or AIM). Yet we must energize this mantra with constant attention. Mere mechanical repetition of a mantra can cause us to lose wakeful awareness and fall into habit. Most important is to remember the deity, guru and higher Self through the mantra the first thing in the morning.[21] This sets the tone of our thoughts for the day.

- Wakeful pranayama – breathing in a deeper energy of consciousness when our minds drift into a lack of awareness. It is a deeper unitary prana that persists in deep sleep. The more we have such a unified and spiritualized prana, the more we can hold a steady awareness throughout the day.

- Contemplative use of the senses – not using the senses at an entertainment or enjoyment level but from a contemplative awareness, learning to be aware of the presence of Being and the light of consciousness responsible for the wonderful forms of nature. This can be developed further into pratyahara, drawing our senses back into the light of awareness within and around us.

- Cultivating a recognition of the impermanence of all waking experience. The apparent solidity and continuity of the waking world is an illusion of the senses. We should note the continual movement of change from the point of changeless consciousness within us, holding to the immutable state of inner wakefulness.

- Recognizing that you are not the body but pure consciousness. The body is located in time and space but your consciousness is beyond time and space. Your body moves but you do not move. Your body has physical features, arms and legs, eyes and ears but you do not. You are the light and energy running the body but not the body itself.

Those who remain perpetually awake never die. Their wakefulness is not rooted in the physical body but in recognition of the Divine presence. To achieve this higher wakefulness requires being undistracted and concentrated in all that we do. Naturally we cannot succeed at this demanding task immediately but we can develop its power gradually day by day. Let every day be a day of greater awakening and expanding wakefulness for you.

Karma Yoga

The waking state is the realm of action or karma, in which our individual and collective karmas come together for a common life experience.

The waking state is characterized by outer actions through the body, motor organs and speech. These begin with necessary bodily functions of eating, breathing and moving and extend to family, work and social activities that occupy most of our waking time. We are acting continually throughout the day. We cannot avoid action but we can act either with awareness or without it. Action with awareness is Yoga. Otherwise action based upon desire breeds not only more karma but keeps us caught in an unaware state where we forget our true nature.

Our action in the waking state should be a form of Karma Yoga or conscious action, performing action with a detached mind aiming at serving the Divine, not gaining any personal rewards. Recognizing that we are not the body, our physical, waking actions are not done for mere personal benefit but to bring greater peace and awareness into the world. True Karma Yoga implies teaching people that their true Self is not the body and that we transcend waking reality, which is a kind of dream and illusion, into a greater wakefulness beyond the body extending to unity with all.

Another aspect of Karma Yoga is the performance of rituals. All action done with regularity and dedication is a kind of ritual, which means a sacred empowerment. Everything that we do should be a ritual or offering to the Divine and sacred presence pervading all life.

If we perform specific rituals during the day, whether worship in the home or temple worship, these can aid in wakeful awareness. Such rituals must be done with consciousness and creativity, not merely compulsively or mechanically. Using awareness enhancing items like incense, flowers, candles and ghee lamps, sacred water and sacred earth or stones helps. Yet our own consciousness is the primary factor.

Karma Yoga should never be done as a mere compulsion. Whatever we do should follow a higher inspiration and be a pursuit of excellence, making all that we do an offering to the Divine and inner Self. If our Karma Yoga is mere drudgery or mindless repetition, it cannot be called Yoga.

Remembering the World of Nature

Nature is one of the greatest powers of the Yoga of the Waking State. We should attune our awareness with the great forces of nature during the day, noting sunrise and sunset, the movement of clouds in the sky, the stars at night or the flowers in the garden. Nature is always present and vibrant, and transformational to the mind, unlike the frequent dullness of our mind and senses. We should remember the sun when we arise in the morning and align our waking awareness with its light.

Nature can provide us with new prana and vitality to remain awake and expansive in our awareness. Underlying nature is the vast cosmic dream and the peace of the cosmic spirit that can help us move with clarity through dream and deep sleep states as well. We can use the awareness of nature to contact the cosmic consciousness or Brahman responsible for it. Nature is Brahman in manifestation. Let us be awake and aware like a mountain, a great river, the ocean or a giant banyan tree. We can hold all outer experiences from the abundance and boundlessness of an inner awareness that connects us with all.

Ayurveda

Ayurveda addresses the healing of the body and mind, and

through it right living as a whole in our waking life. It recommends certain herbs for promoting and sustaining wakefulness like brahmi, manduka parni, ashwagandha, calamus and shankha pushpi. Mint based teas like sage, mint (pudina) or tulsi (holy basil) can also help.[22]

Sustaining wakefulness is easier when the food we eat is natural and full of prana, when we do not overeat and weigh the body down. It requires that the nervous system is properly hydrated with herbal beverages and fruit juices. It requires regular exercise, particularly walking in nature, but also asana and pranayama. Bathing and swimming can be very helpful. These help remove inertia from the body.

Recognizing that we are not the body does not mean that we neglect or abuse the body. On the contrary, we come to better appreciate the body as a tool of higher consciousness, a means of bringing Divine energies into our lives. We should honor the body as nature's gift of experience to us and respect its natural rhythms and organic intelligence. This means to keep our bodies wakefully attuned to nature, its energies and its transformations. Understanding and adapting to our individual Ayurvedic mind-body constitution or doshic type is very helpful for this.

The Yoga of the Dream State

Dream is much more mysterious than the waking state, suggesting hidden secrets of the soul and higher realms of imagination and inspiration. Yet we seldom seriously explore the dream state, though we are all enticed by dreams in various ways. Clearly there is much about dreams that we would like to know, including the ultimate identity of the dreamer. The Yoga of the Dream State teaches us how to use dreams to fulfill our deepest wishes and take us beyond desire as well.

From the standpoint of the waking state, we regard the dream state as unreal and largely unimportant, as the waking statement of "it was only a dream" reflects. We find our dreams to be interesting or even fascinating but usually only for a few minutes after we wake up in the morning. Only a few dreams leave a lasting imprint on us, though they usually remain enigmatic.

Most dream patterns seem meaningless or at best some vague intimation. Sometimes we have very happy dreams that make our waking life seem dismal. Other times we have disturbed dreams that may make us afraid of the dream state and apprehensive to ever enter into it.

All of us have been profoundly affected by the power of bad dreams, extending to nightmares, which upset our psychology and agitate our nervous systems. Similarly, we all have experienced colorful and entrancing dreams that we wish were real and would like to continue as our true reality. The dream state has its effects, particularly at a psychological level that we should not underestimate, just as our thoughts affect our health.

Modern psychoanalysis starting with Sigmund Freud examines the dream state as an important part of its diagnosis and treatment. Yet Freudian psychology has utterly failed to explore the depths of dreaming and the mysteries of the deeper consciousness that dwells behind the dream state. It proposes that dreams are merely reflections of the urges and traumas of the waking state, particularly sexuality and childhood experiences, and not any connection to higher states of consciousness. Modern psychology explores what it calls the subconscious and unconscious, which are lesser states of awareness, but has little understanding of the deeper layers of consciousness behind waking, dream and deep sleep. It has only addressed the superficial levels of the mind and the dreaming process, not the deeper layers of cosmic awareness.

Most psychoanalysis prefers to examine the garbage heap of old experiences and their fermentation in dreams, rather than looking at the creative vision behind dreaming or its possible other levels of meaning. The exception is the types of psychology rooted in the work of C.G. Jung, which connect dream to the collective unconscious or even higher states of consciousness, as well as to a higher creativity. Yet even with Jungian psychology there is not the understanding of higher states of consciousness (samadhi) and Self-realization that we find in the Vedic traditions. Yoga and Vedanta take us to a deeper understanding dream and consciousness overall, leading us to the universal Self, not simply to personal or collective dreams and their implications.

Dream, Imagination and Desire

Dreaming as an activity of the mind is connected to the imagination of the waking state, what is called *vikalpa* in the *Yoga Sutras.*[23] Yoga regards vikalpa as a state of false imagination, like imagining horns on a rabbit. Yet ultimately Yoga regards all the movements of the mind, including waking and sleep, as types of vikalpa or as involving some degree of false imagination or distorted perception. This is because all mental activity is tinged with some sort of wishful thinking. Yoga aims ultimately at the state of *Nirvikalpa Samadhi,* Samadhi or unity consciousness without any vikalpas – the mind in the state of mirror-like wisdom, with no disturbances of imagination or desire.

Overall our minds are motivated by desire (kama), which creates fantasy, leading to dreaming or imagining the fulfillment of desire, even in the waking state. We often find that waking life proceeds too slowly and does not provide the immediate wish fulfillment that we seek; so we simply imagine such fulfillment occurring. This imagination, although not real, gives a degree of pleasure and satisfaction, even at a physical level. Such pleasurable escapes from the drudgery of life make the realm of imagination and dream a fascinating past time throughout the day. For many of us fantasy and imagination is more important than our waking reality. We love our fantasies, even if we are never able to fulfill them in real life.

Drugs, Technology and the Dream State

Today the new information technology with its "virtual reality" is providing a stronger dreamlike power of projection, which can be more vivid than our own imagination as it can be made palpable to the senses. Soon people may prefer this new virtual reality made possible by the miracles of technology as it can better fulfill our many desires than physical reality, which moves slowly with much resistance. Many of us find enjoyment in movies or stories in which we gain a kind of wish fulfillment by our identification with the characters involved. Clearly fantasy has a tremendous value for us, dominating even the waking state as well as providing the basis for our dreams.

The use of mind-altering plants and drugs to enhance the imagination is another method with a long history going back to prehistoric times and several traditional cultures. It is now enhanced further with a new technology. This new extensive pharmaceutical knowledge has created many new mind-altering and mind-controlling drugs, now available through medical treatment or as recreational drugs (which may be illegal).

Drugs are external substances to control our minds and stimulate our imagination and senses. The use of such drugs is widespread and often has depleting effects both on our nervous systems and bodies. Drugs also can create long-lasting issues with the physical nervous system, endocrine system and the nervous sheath and leave behind obstacles that can take years to resolve. To the extent they have artificially forced experiences onto the mind, they sometimes also lead to serious psychological imbalances that can warp the perceptions of the physical world in ways that can be harmful as well.

We can use mind-altering drugs to heighten our experience into dream-like states even during waking reality. Intoxicants starting with alcohol can make us feel better about ourselves or the world around us. Opiates for pain relief can also promote sleep and dream, and cause many severe addictions. There are many types of sedatives and sleeping pills to promote sleep for those who cannot fall asleep easily, though these may not improve our dreams and may depress our creative intelligence.

Psychedelics, hallucinogenics and new designer drugs can push us into more powerful dream-like states or even trances. Some people regard them as aids to meditation. Even the *Yoga Sutras* mentions the lower samadhis that can arise through the use of herbs or drugs.[24]

We find a sacred use of plants in traditional societies and

among shamans as aids in the spiritual quest, but this is a matter of great discretion and preparation, not merely self-indulgence. Such mind-altering plants are best as initiatory tools to be used sparingly and in a sacred manner. Yet we find many people with modern life-styles indulging in them regularly for escape, entertainment or as a new high, in which cases they are of little value and can cause harm.

As substances from the outside, drugs and pharmaceutical agents easily breed dependency and encourage illusion. Used wrongly, mind-altering drugs can damage the subtle or energy body, causing problems that are beyond treatment at a physical or psychological level, and disrupting the inner connection with our higher Self.

Art, Vision Quests and Meditation

We need not rely upon technology to heighten dream experiences. As our minds develop and we gain create powers of concentration and visualization, we can easily have more vivid dreams as a consequence.

The connection between dream and art is well known. Artists intentionally cultivate their imagination and subtle sensory refinement, sometimes directly through inspiration, sometimes indirectly with drugs and intoxicants or unusual behavior that may end up disturbing them. Refining our awareness allows us to see the subtle energy patterns in nature that are quite artistic with its subtle designs and gestalts. Artists learn to see patterns of dream energies behind waking reality, as in symbolic and surrealistic art.

Vision quests, such as we find in shamanic cultures, are another way to access the dream state and its learning potentials. Many native peoples are more connected to the dream state, as with the Australian aborigines who are said to live in dreamtime, not in waking reality. While we tend to look down upon such groups as primitive, the dream world can provide a wisdom and happiness far beyond the limited waking state that we know, and certainly a greater knowledge of the world of nature, which has its subtle dream reality as well as its waking reality.

Meditation naturally results in a heightened power of vision and creative imagination, a greater sensitivity to light and color, as well as a recognition of the presence of space. Meditation can provide a power of visualization that can help bring higher dreams and wishes into manifestation. Meditators may receive special dream teachings or dream messages that provide a deeper level of guidance and inspiration.

Ancient and medieval cultures had a greater power of dreaming and imagining than we do today. Some of these, like visions of heaven and hell can be extreme. Yet mystical and devotional images can reflect greater realities and deeper insights; such as the unusual iconography in ancient temples. Yogic art portrays deities with animal heads or bodies, multiple arms or legs, or other symbolic depictions that like dreams can communicate to the deeper mind where the power of the image prevails over verbal expression.

Developing dream wisdom, the power of imagination and visualization, has an important place in healing the body and mind and in the development of higher awareness. What we imagine in our minds precedes and structures our outer physical reality. In this regard rather than a mere reflection of the waking state, dreams and positive imagination can be a means of improving our physical life and wellbeing. The outer world is more a manifestation of our inner thoughts, than our dreams being simply an imagination arising from waking state memories.

Dream Worlds and the Astral Plane

Yoga teaches us that there is an entire dream world and dream self that has its own existence and identity. Dreams may not just be our own imagination but may also connect us to the astral plane that is its own realm of existence beyond the physical.

Besides your waking self and its waking world, you have another deeper and subtler dream self and dream world. The dream self is related to the waking self and its experiences but as enhanced by a potential power of vision, imagination and creativity. The dream world or astral plane is called the subtle world as compared with the heavier gross physical world. The astral world is full of light and life but variable and quickly changing in form and expression.

Unlike physical reality that is dense and fixed, dream reality is fluid and malleable, easily influenced by thoughts and emotions. The mental and emotional ups and downs that are hidden behind the gross physical body manifest directly in the dream body, creating our dream world and its shifting currents that can be either exalting or frightening.

If we are not in control of our minds, our dream reality can easily turn into bad dreams and nightmares. This is why less evolved souls prefer the physical world, which is steadier and not as directly affected by our thoughts. They lack the self-control and mind control necessary to function in the subjective thought created reality of the dream worlds. Yet if we can control our thoughts, we can visualize meetings with great masters and exalted deities and contact them within, if we are sincere. Whatever we wish for must eventually bear fruit, but only to the extent we wholeheartedly energize it.

Just as the waking state vibrates to the forces of the waking world, the dream state vibrates according to the dream world and its subtler currents. While in the waking state we work with an objective world born of collective karma, in the dream state we work with a subjective world based on our own thoughts and imaginations.

This subjective dream realm can have its own reality and connections with other beings and creatures. We may visit the astral world in dreams if we have enough awareness to be able to move beyond mere personal dreams to the greater dream reality of cosmic creation.

Our dream aspirations and deepest wishes should go together. There is much that we are not able to accomplish within the limited parameters of physical reality. The dream realm contains our vision of the future, including discovering happiness, love, peace and fulfillment.

However, if our minds are not pure, the dream state can degenerate into illusions that involve connections with lower astral worlds of turbulence, violence, anger, and hatred. These extend to asuric realms and to realms of the departed, ghosts and other dangerous psychic forces.

If we are in control of our minds, on the other hand, we will resonate with the higher astral worlds of art, devotion and Divine love. There are vast astral realms of art, vision, inspiration and joy. Cultivating artistic expression can help us access the higher levels of the dream state. This can lead us to yet higher form realms of Divine love, bliss and devotion, the Deva Lokas or Divine realms of Bhakti Yoga.

In the dream state we have access to the subtle elements or *tanmatras*, the creative essences underlying the sensory potentials of sound, touch, sight, taste and smell. The sensory potentials of the dream state are vaster and more refined than those of the waking state, but require cultivation of the mind and a purer perception to appreciate.

Our dream or astral soul comes to the front after death, as the radiance or afterglow of our physical lives. We only touch this astral light superficially during physical existence, though some souls retain a strong astral experience even on Earth. They may become artists, mystics, occultists and psychics, using their astral powers and sensitivities.

The astral body is made of light and energy, life and prana. It is much more variable than the physical body and can change shape, size and appearance with relative ease, according to our will, thought and emotions.

The astral world has its own language, which is one of symbols, images and mantras. This includes colors, forms, gestures, aromas, chants and music much more subtle and beautiful than those of the physical world. This makes communication with other astral creatures easy and largely telepathic, a realm overflowing with deep expressions and profound associations.

You can discover your dream landscape and the dream stories, once you learn to connect to your dream life. You can learn to map out your dream world and dreamtime, its various realms of experience and your activities within them. You can conduct a dream search for higher potentials within you. There are dream treasures that your dream self is collecting in terms of dream objects of beauty, wisdom, creative insight and delight, like special astral gems and flowers that nothing merely physical can compare to.

Your associations in the waking state may continue, change or disappear in your dream life. You may find new friends and teachers in the dream world, including creatures other than humans. You may discover dream animals or dream sages, and have new experiences, powers and realizations far beyond your waking capacities. Or you may find different aspects of your waking associates active in the dream state, in different forms or taking different roles relative to you.

The astral or dream world is much more vivid, wondrous and delightful than the physical world. It is filled with life and vision and has a liquid quality to it, ever flowing. The light of the astral dawn is particularly beautiful. It ushers us into dream worlds of beauty, light and splendor.

There are great colorful astral mountains and wide astral rivers and seas. The astral world has the most extraordinary plants and trees with massive leaves and flowers, like a great tropical paradise, overflowing on every side. Inspiring astral gardens exist, cultivated with love devotion. Fountains of happiness and delight can be found, spreading out into formless worlds beyond. The higher astral realms have beautiful astral temples, sustained by Divine thoughts. There are many astral or dream heavens, the paradises in which all wishes are fulfilled.

Dream visions and vision quests are part of many occult and spiritual paths. They may involve facing our fears personified as various evil spirits, demons, and wild animals. Most heavens of religious striving can be found in the astral plane. These are realms of good karma, good deeds, good thoughts, charity, kindness and compassion. Yet in the lower astral realms illusory heavens or realms of religious delusions also occur, extending into realms of false imagination of every possible type.

We must remember that all such astral realms are transient and represent another type of temporary experience for the soul in its journey through the universe of consciousness. The higher astral realms form the gateway to realms of pure spiritual knowledge and the powers of cosmic creation. The lower astral planes have more illusions than the waking state, as there is no waking reality to measure them against.

The astral plane is not an end in itself but a step to the formless world. It can certainly bring us much more enjoyments and a sense of beauty and wonder than the dense physical realm, but these may breed new and more powerful attachments if we are not careful.

Working with our Dream Reality

There are many methods that we can explore to work with and change our dream reality. There are mundane, intellectual or artistic approaches that remain at a mental level. There are also higher methods that are yogic and meditational, using mantra and prana as well. These levels can overlap to some degree. We can classify these dream approaches according to several types.

> The first involve the science or science fiction idea of getting into peoples minds and manipulating their dreams. This may be drug induced or by manipulating brain waves, or by hypnosis. Yet such approaches are rooted in taking the waking state to be real and are still caught in physical reality. Their side effects can be dangerous.
>
> Second are occultists who pursue astral travel, waking and moving in the dream state and the astral world. They learn certain special methods, formulas, mantras or pranayamas to awaken and move into the astral body. They realize the reality of the dream state and through practice may gain various psychic abilities. Yet they are usually caught in a subtle ego, illusion and false imagination, which are considerable in the dream realm of desire, which has a force of Maya greater than the Maya of the physical realm.

Third are meditation approaches that teach us how to work with our dreams in order to transcend the outer idea of who we are and the move beyond the material world. This is what deeper yogic practices teach us. Some yogis learn to awaken in the subtle or dream body and visit the subtle worlds for higher knowledge and experience, without being trapped in its illusions. There are astral ashrams and temples that we may visit for higher knowledge and deeper education. Other yogis may simply awaken in dream and move beyond the dream worlds, going directly into formless levels of awareness beyond any imagination that relate more to the state of deep sleep.

Mastering the Power of Imagination and Visualization

Imagination or vikalpa is the main mental function that we need to master in order to understand and go beyond the dream state. There are two basic ways to do this.

1) We expand our imagination into the infinite
   – this is the positive route or way of affirmation.

2) We negate our imagination altogether into nothingness
   – this is the negative route or way of negation.

Tantric yogis usually follow the first method or way of affirmation in which they cultivate their power of visualization and imagination in a spiritual direction. This is accomplished by visualizing deities, higher lokas, or mystical images, symbols and processes, including the chakras of the subtle body that belong to the astral plane. We find such many practices in Hindu Tantra and in Buddhist Tantra, particularly in Kundalini Yoga.

Most Jnanis, who follow the Yoga of Knowledge, follow the second approach or way of negation. This involves holding to the formless clear light of awareness as the ultimate truth and rejecting every form of imagination as unreal, including visions of deities or higher worlds.

The two approaches may be intertwined or followed one after the other. After the power of imagination is cultivated consciously, it can more easily be negated. Cultivating the power of imagination is usually preparatory or constitutes the gradual path. Direct insight is usually the higher or direct path. The path of imagination and visualization is more properly part of the Dream Yoga, while the way of negation is more related to the formless Yogas beyond.

Yet we must always be careful, even in higher astral realms, to not get caught in fantasies and illusions. The Maya of dream and the astral worlds is very powerful and very hard to overcome. We feel compelled to emphasize this point owing to the many possible dangers involved in the astral plane, extending from hypnosis to possession.

Yoga Practices of the Dream State

The practice of Yoga continues from the waking into the dream state but more at the level of the mind. There are many ways to do this. To facilitate it, it requires first developing the right intention and regular practice, as well as support practices, in the waking state. The dream state reflects the motivation of the waking mind, taking it inward.

There are two primary aspects of the Yoga of the Dream State, much like the two ways of expanding or negating our imagination:

> The first involves trying to wake up in the dream state, which usually brings our dreams to an end. This does not mean having our waking ego become aware in the

dream state. Instead it means contacting the witness consciousness in both waking and dream, detached from both body and mind. Once we recognize we are dreaming, we can negate the dream experience into pure awareness. This relates to the Yoga of Knowledge.

The second is to dream our highest spiritual dreams and aspirations, which is closely connected to Bhakti Yoga. It is to cultivate the higher powers of imagination, which are the visionary capacities of the mind, to reflect a higher spiritual reality. These include Tantric methods of visualizing deities, yantras, chakras and energy centers within us, which are located in the subtle body.

Yoga of Conscious Dreaming

The Yoga of conscious dreaming is based upon maintaining a clear awareness during dream, of being aware that we are dreaming. This allows us to transform our dreams and turn them into tools of deeper insight. We strive to awake in the dream state and then play with the dream, recognizing it as a creation of our own minds. We learn to change the forms and experience of the dream or take the dream forward in a spiritual direction of beauty and bliss.

The wakeful awareness of the waking state can be continued into the dream state, but its nature changes. When we wake within the dream state the dream may come to an end and form a deeper entrance into the state of deep sleep. We then have the choice to either move on to a deeper state of waking or to move more consciously into deep sleep. This Yoga of conscious dreaming is a continuation of the wakeful Yoga of the waking state. But it requires that we let go of our physical identity. It is not the physical body or ego that practices the true dream Yoga; it is the inner awareness or higher mind that does so.

Pranayama and the Energy Body of Dream

The dream world forms energy field and reflects our aura. The dream body includes our energy body or pranic sheath. Pranayama helps us energize the dream or subtle body and its different channels or nadis. Pranayama helps liberate the dream body from its attachment to the physical body. The dream body manifests as we develop the state of kumbhaka, the yogic holding of the breath, by the power of consciousness.

Those who practice pranayama with concentration and awareness can easily master the dream state. They may have more vivid dreams and experience themselves as flying within the dream state. We can use the power of prana to move through the dream worlds and alter our dream reality at will.

We can awaken the five pranas at an astral or dream level:

- Ascending in consciousness through Udana Vayu that moves upward.
- Descending and grounding our awareness through Apana Vayu that moves downward.
- Expanding our awareness through Vyana Vayu that moves us to the periphery.
- Centering our awareness through Samana Vayu that draws us to the center.
- These must be energized with an overall higher power of Prana that comes through surrendering our vitality to the Divine will within us.

The Dream State, Subtle Body and Chakras

Most chakra work and Kundalini Yoga occurs from the level of the astral plane, connected to the awakened dream state. The chakras are part of the awakened subtle body, most notably the five lower chakras that relate to the five sensory potentials and the five elements, and especially the heart chakra as the seat of devotion.

Yoga practices involving the chakras include working with the astral realm and its connections to the deeper causal realm. Yet the highest chakras, the third eye and lotus of the head, also connect us to the true Self beyond all manifestation.

In order to open the chakras, we must first visualize them clearly in the subtle body, along with their corresponding Sanskrit letters, mantras, colors, deities and element connections. There are many yogic tools for doing this in various methods of Kundalini Yoga, particularly in Tantric texts, including those of Hatha Yoga and those that aim at the worship of the Goddess or Shakti.

Kundalini Shakti both energizes the dream plane as well as ultimately taking us beyond it. That is why it is often a force of illusion in our initial experiences that can disturb the mind or even the nervous system as well, as many have experienced in Shaktipat transmissions.

The power of imagination is ultimately the power of cosmic creation. Many Yogis get caught in the illusions of the chakras and forget that *we are not the chakras or the subtle body, any more than we are the physical body and its organs.* They may remain trapped in the astral worlds instead of continuing into the pure Self.

The Dream State and Bhakti Yoga

You should pursue your highest dreams in life, which are to commune with the greater universe within our own hearts, worshipping the Divine in the form that your heart most aspires to. This is the basis of Bhakti Yoga, the Yoga of Divine Love.

The higher dream state is a realm of devotion and Bhakti Yoga, particularly the worship of the Divine in various forms. The various deity depictions of Hindu art, with multiple heads and supernatural powers are visions of the higher realms of the dream state. The Deva lokas are on the higher astral plane. We can access these through conscious dreaming. Yet we should not pursue them directly but allow them to manifest as a consequence of a deepening devotion.

Dream is the best state in which to dream our highest dream, which, if we go to the core of our hearts and the eternal wishes of our souls, is that of communion with the deity in divine realms of pure energy, light and happiness. Bhakti Yoga has a special resonance with the higher aspects of the dream state.

Devotional music, mantra and chanting transform the dream state into a natural state of yogic worship. Many astral beings sing rather than talk. Music and dance are part of their ordinary expression. Many of what are called angels in western thought or devas in Hindu thought are contacts with these astral light beings at various levels.

Mantra Yoga is one of the key practices of Dream Yoga, particularly chanting the names of deities like OM Namah Shivaya or the names of gurus, in order to connect with them in the dream worlds. Mantra is the language of the higher astral worlds.

Creative visualization is very helpful in the Dream Yoga, particularly visualizing the Divine with our inner eye, in a male or female form, with various ornaments or weapons, and in special attire. The practice of *manasa puja* or mind-based puja is excellent for spiritualizing the dream state. In this puja, one visualizes the worship of the deity in the heart with imaginary flowers, lights and offerings. Such dream rituals can be very elaborate, colorful and dramatic.

As you fall asleep, call to mind the image of the deity and commune with it according to your vision and your aspiration. The deity will take the form that best communicates with you. You can do the same with the guru. Guru Yoga is another Yoga of the dream state, with astral communication with the teacher at a telepathic level.

Siddhis of the Dream State

There are many special powers that one can experience in the dream state that has a more adaptable reality than the waking state. One can learn the art of astral travel to different astral worlds, or move in the astral body to other physical locations and observe them at a subtle level. This is what many psychics do and this forms the source of their special extrasensory knowledge. Some astrologers do the same.

Astral flying is easy as the dream body is light and airy, unlike the heavy physical body, which is often experienced by those adept at Pranayama. The siddhis of the dream state include an ability to make the dream body as large or small as we wish, as heavy or light, as fast or slow in movement, or take whatever form we wish, much like the power of Lord Hanuman. We can also fulfill our desires on the astral plane by the power of Divine love alone. The traditional eight siddhis of Yoga are largely those of the subtle body.

Yet the highest siddhi of the dream world and the astral plane involves viveka, the discernment not to take any dream images or astral forms as real, and to move beyond them to pure awareness. We must develop detachment even from the spiritual beauties of the higher astral plane and its heavenly realms. This is only possible when we understand the light of consciousness illuminating these wonderful colors. However entrancing the dream state, it is but a gateway to a deeper formless awareness.

The Yoga of Deep Sleep

Deep sleep is the point of return of our daily cycle in which it renews itself. Deep sleep is the beginning and end of our lives and the basis of all our time cycles. It is like the womb where the mind returns at night and re-emerges in the morning. It is not just a matter of needing the rest of deep sleep at a biological and organic level. There is a greater spiritual necessity to deep sleep and the mystery of the soul that it reflects. Deep sleep is our doorway to the cosmic reality. The Yoga of Deep Sleeps teaches us how to open that door.

Deep sleep is necessary to sustain both body and mind. Without it the body loses its energy, vitality and immunity and the mind loses its peace, clarity and power of attention. Yet deep sleep also holds the keys to the rejuvenation and transcendence of body and mind, which are rarely known or applied. These are some of the spiritual secrets of Yoga and Ayurveda.

We still do not truly know what happens in the state of deep sleep, either in terms of our personal experience, or in terms of current medicine, science, philosophy or religion, though we undergo this state every day.

First of all, we need deep sleep because waking reality is a kind of agitation and disturbance, a state of friction that wears us out and causes our prana to dissipate. *Waking life is artificial and unnatural to the soul, and it must return to the state of deep sleep in order to contact its true wellsprings of vitality and awareness.*

Life energy or Prana is foreign to physical or material reality and only exists if sustained by complex organic processes, particularly breathing, food and water. Deep sleep allows the inner Prana to renew the outer prana at a physical level. Yet this Prana of deep sleep is not well understood. It is ultimately not physical at all, but the very energy of Consciousness.

Even the dream state, though having a subtler pranic force than the waking state, has its transience and artificiality and can also wear out our energies in its rapid movements and expressions. We also need deep sleep to renew our powers of perception and creative imagination. Proper deep sleep supports restful, happy and inspiring dreams.

Most importantly, inner transformations that occur during deep sleep are necessary for the greater evolution of the soul, though unlike waking and dream we may not be aware of their movements. Our waking experience is not the only important factor in our spiritual growth. Our inner work continues in dream and deep sleep, not only as an extension of waking but as a process in its own right. In deep sleep we experience the fruit of our spiritual practice as an ability to move beyond the darkness of manifest existence. Cultivating awareness in deep sleep is more transformative than any practices we do in the waking and dream states.

Our personal waking state is a state of spiritual sleep and ignorance. The soul that sleeps in the waking state is able to awaken in deep sleep, and allow its energy to come forth to refresh the constricted waking life. Subtle changes in our karmic patterns occur in sleep that affect our actions for the following day.

Deep sleep allows us to absorb and digest experiences from the waking state, which would otherwise clog and clutter our minds and inhibit us from new experiences of life. Deep sleep empties the mind of its residues for another day of new activities. Deep sleep is not only a blank state but also a state of negation that removes what is unnecessary or obstructive to our energy flow – a clearinghouse for the mind. If we do not bring awareness into the state of deep sleep, it will serve only as a container for karmic patterns, impulsions and illusions and only remove superficial thoughts.

Nature of Deep Sleep

What is the nature of deep sleep? Ordinarily we experience it as simply a blank feeling or emptiness but as we bring awareness into it, deep sleep reveals seed potentials, sound patterns, special vibrations and energy currents, though inchoate. Deep sleep is not static but has a movement into itself, like waves on the sea. It forms the background pattern of awareness prior to the emergence of defined thoughts. Sparks are there, tendencies of waking and dream; deep currents are there, including from other lives, other creatures and other worlds. Deep sleep is a place of pure potential. One can experience not simply actual phenomena but the essence of all things possible as one becomes aware at this deep level.

Sometimes the state of deep sleep is metaphorically described as a cavern. It resembles a dark and enclosed limited space or tunnel like a cave. When illuminated with the light of awareness, we discover it has its own growth and life; much like the stalactites, stalagmites, water currents and even hidden gems of a cave. Moving through deep sleep is like traveling through the different chambers of such a cavern; some vast, some narrow, none easy to illuminate, some hard to enter, but many containing profound secrets and hidden passageways to other realms.

As one consciously moves through the state of deep sleep, one learns to navigate through its dark clouds of unknowing and occasional lightning flashes of higher insight. Deep sleep holds a tremendous power reserve and capacity, though half suspended. There is a persistent awareness in deep sleep, a kind of primal reality, yet extending to an unknown transcendence, a light at the top of the cavern towards which one can ascend beyond all darkness. Deep sleep holds all the latent powers of nature, all the possibilities of the soul's unfoldment, and the seeds of all the challenges that we must eventually face.

Deep sleep is the seed state of our being, in which we can experience the cosmos in its seed form prior to the differentiation of creaturely expressions. In the Brihadaranyaka Upanishad[25]:

- The waking state is related to this world or the Earth
- Deep sleep to the Heaven or the world beyond
- With dream as their juncture in the atmosphere

In Deep sleep we touch the realm of Heaven as our original abode in the space of pure consciousness. The waking state is our familiar Earth and the dream state is the turbulent atmosphere.

The deep sleep state connects us with the powers of the night, the stars and the vast expanse of the night sky. We can expand into the cosmos through the state of deep sleep. Yogis learn to work with these cosmic powers of night, sleep, silence, solitude and transcendence. In this higher darkness, the mind and heart are renewed, and limiting constructs of time and space simply dissolve. This dark night of deep sleep holds the night Sun, the hidden Self of cosmic illumination, which we can unfold at the core of our being to reveal the magical nature of all existence.

Yoga in the State of Deep Sleep and Samadhi

Compared to the tangibility of the Yoga of the waking state and its connection to the physical body, and to the astral images of the Yoga of the dream state and its connection to the subtle body, the Yoga of deep sleep initially appears very obscure, difficult and hidden, like groping blindly in the dark. Should one be able to develop awareness in the state of deep sleep, bringing recognition of that to the waking state is very hard to maintain.

We should remember that traditional Yoga is defined as *samadhi*, a mysterious term often identified with a state of trance or ecstasy that removes us from physical functioning. More accurately, samadhi is the silent and merged state of the mind – the mind turned within and absorbed into its inner nature of pure awareness. In the samadhi state the mind functions like a mirror to reveal things as they are, no longer coloring them by its own conditioned movements. In higher samadhis there are no thoughts at all but simply consciousness resting in its own being. The potential of everything is there but no specific form is as yet revealed.

Deep sleep, as already noted, is our natural samadhi that all creatures have access to and are entitled to as part of their natural existence. This means that moving consciously into deep sleep constitutes the easiest access to the state of samadhi, the goal of Yoga that all yoga practitioners should seek to benefit from. Awareness in deep sleep can be made into natural Yoga of Samadhi. As such, awareness in deep sleep can take us immediately into the highest limb of Yoga practice.

Yet the samadhi of deep sleep has a tamasic quality in the ordinary person. It reflects samadhi like qualities of peace and happiness, in which the mind can become renewed, but we do not recognize its deeper nature and power or know how to benefit from it directly. Deep sleep is like a barrier that we cannot cross over without losing ourselves. The Yoga of deep sleep requires shining the light of awareness into this darkness. When so illuminated, it changes its nature and reveals its secrets and connections to the universe as a whole.

By way of contrast, the dream state involves imagination or vikalpa and usually keeps us caught in the mind. Deep sleep can more easily lead us to the higher Nirvikalpa state or Samadhi beyond the imaginative mind as in it the imaginative mind is reduced to its core energy. Like Samadhi, deep sleep is a state of nirodha, in which there is a control or negation of the disturbances of the mind. It is a kind of unconscious or half-conscious Nirvana in which we can move beyond all dualities and desires.

The Yoga of deep sleep requires that we remain aware inwardly in the deep sleep state, with body and mind at rest but our inner consciousness awake and observant. This is only possible if we are detached from body and mind and their ongoing fears and desires in our daily lives. Waking up in the state of deep sleep means waking from the dream of physical reality, leaving the darkness of spiritual ignorance for the light of knowledge, and moving beyond the dream illusion of the mind to the pure light of Being. It requires transcending all dreams and wishes to a state of inner contentment and peace beyond any wants or cravings.

The Yoga of deep sleep relates to the Yoga of the spiritual heart (hridaya). It requires merging our outer sensory faculties into the light of the spiritual heart that is their essence and origin. This is only possible when we have a one-pointed mind and focused prana, and when our inner eye and inner prana are open and expanding. The light of deep sleep dwells in the spiritual heart. Merging the mind into the deeper heart takes us through and beyond the state of deep sleep to the true Self within.

Our ability to remain conscious in deep sleep requires an ability to be alone, not only physically but also mentally and emotionally. It rests upon inner silence, which is not just absence of speech but silence of mind. It requires that we dwell in a formless state beyond sensory perception, letting go of the need for any external vision, object or event to engage us. We must be willing to abide in space, voidness and emptiness, to become nothing and let go of any sense of the reality in the material and form worlds.

The Self that is responsible for deep sleep is the individual soul or Jivatman, the reincarnating being within us. It is our hidden, secret or forgotten identity transcending the body and mind of waking and dream realities that constitute the cycle of birth and death. Contacting the Self of deep sleep allows us to understand our soul's purpose and karma, to connect with the soul's memory and recognition according to its motivation or samkalpa.

Becoming conscious at a soul level, which means becoming conscious of our true nature as an immortal being, is the key to waking up in the state of deep sleep. When we are conscious of ourselves as an immortal spiritual being, having many bodies and lives, we are already waking up to our true reality underlying waking, dream and deep sleep. Yet that spiritual being has no form other than the light of awareness.

Dangers of the State of Deep Sleep

The Yoga of deep sleep can be arduous and dangerous. It requires great patience and tenacity, facing and going beyond the monumental ignorance and darkness at the root of our transient existence. It requires passing through the dark night of the soul, the unknowing that negates the conditioned knowledge of the outer mind.

The Yoga of deep sleep demands that we dive deep into the root of the unconscious mind and all of its chaotic subterranean fears and primeval desires – cutting through them, slaying the dragon, as it were, at the foundation of this world of illusion. As such, the Yoga of deep sleep leads us to the transcendent Yoga of direct realization and forms its first phase. This requires fearlessness and tremendous discernment or viveka. To move through our inner darkness, letting go of body and mind, means the death of the ego and all that we are attached to.

If our awareness is not focused and determined, we easily get trapped in certain blank states of mind, emptiness or latency and do not make the real leap into transcendence. These are among the shadowy states connected to deep sleep. Such states of mergence into this primal state of latency are found in yogic literature.[26] Even time and space are lost there, though eternity and infinity cannot manifest fully either. The true guru does not allow the disciple to get caught in the false peace and state of mergence of these unmanifest but still not fully aware states, but directs the disciple further to the supreme light of awareness. Yet in that darkness we might not easily hear the guru's vibratory voice.

Formless Awareness

The Yoga of Deep Sleep is based on abiding in formless awareness, returning back to the original void or state of emptiness in which everything is hidden in seed form. In deep sleep there is neither any objective world to be perceived, nor any separate self who could perceive it. Both the world and self-consciousness are merged in a state of pure potential, which possesses only currents of possibilities and background patterns of underlying forces that will eventually manifest but as yet have no distinct characteristics.

This formless awareness is like a mass of light, energy, and vibration with only an incipient movement not yet taking any specific indications. There is no outer or form based bodily self and its conditions or worldly objects for it to contact. Being conscious of this root vibration underlying all forms is the foundation the Yoga of Deep Sleep.

In deep sleep there is a mergence into the heart, in which we all feel peace, rest and gain the capacity for renewal. Yet we are not aware of ourselves in this state, but only hold its essence or rasa. We awake feeling we have slept well, but do not remember exactly why or what we have experienced. We must learn to taste that sense of having slept well back to the essence of our being underlying the mind. It is not the biological contentment of sleep that we are reflecting but the blissful peace of our own inner being.

We must learn to let go of name and form, body and mind and rest in the undifferentiated state of awareness that is the substratum even of deep sleep. We must accept the great mystery that true knowledge transcends the mind and that what the mind knows is just a form of darkness or ignorance that can at best reflect some limited aspect of the light. Then deep sleep can lead us into the Turiya state, as its darkness turns into a secret light.

Anandamaya Kosha: The Bliss Sheath and the Causal Plane

Deep sleep is the realm of Anandamaya kosha or the bliss sheath, in which we naturally experience the happiness that is our true nature. Anandamaya kosha affords us access to Savikalpa Samadhis or the limited Samadhis of yogic thought, which are the main samadhis experienced as long as subtle karmic latencies remain. Such imagination based Samadhis that are possible in the waking and dream states rest upon their seed that persists in deep sleep.[27] In deep sleep we unconsciously fall into this Anandamaya state. In higher Yoga practices we learn to bring this Anandamaya function consciously into all aspects of our lives, bringing an inner joy into all that we do.

There are higher formless worlds above the form worlds of the dream state, or what is called the "causal plane", that can be perceived by sustaining awareness in deep sleep. These are realms of meditation,[28] formless space, voidness and light. They allow us to experience infinity in various aspects, dimensions and articulations, including the laws through which the universe operates (what is called Mahat Tattva in yogic thought). We may explore these by accessing the formless awareness at the core of our being, a higher mind without the need for any external world or body.

We can learn to perceive higher causal principles of unity and harmony, the rule of cosmic law and principles prior to the existence of any specific forms. One way to do this is to meditate upon the yantras or geometrical forms of the deities, like the famous Sri Yantra that manifests out of OM to encompass the entire universe. The causal plane is the realm of both cosmic law and the seed mantras that hold them. As we become awake in the deep sleep state, its dark currents take shape as the archetypal patterns of the causal realm of pure creative intelligence. We can learn to focus the dark clouds of deep sleep into profound energy patterns, in which their inherent lightning comes forth in great illuminations of cosmic knowledge.

The Yoga of deep sleep develops a formless awareness that takes us back to the hidden energies responsible for all existence. It requires a meditative immersion that concentrates our awareness back into the origin of all that is. As such it becomes a realm of contemplation, not of mere blankness of mind as in the ordinary deep sleep state.

Different Aspects of the Yoga of Deep Sleep

The Yoga of Deep Sleep develops on two primary levels, which are both aspects of Yoga Nidra or yogic sleep in the real sense of the term.

- First, the Yoga of Deep Sleep can occur in the waking state from the practice of deep pratyahara, sensory concentration and sensory withdrawal. It is possible to focus the mind, prana and senses into a condition of waking deep sleep, as a unity of perception turned within. One holds one's awareness deep within the heart and the outer mind and senses are shut off.

- Second, the Yoga of Deep Sleep occurs in deep sleep state by maintaining a continual awareness. One is aware in the state of deep sleep not as the waking mind, but as the deeper state of seeing observing the mind. This is the true Yoga Nidra or yogic sleep of higher awareness, which is mergence back into the source of reality. It is here that the Yoga of Deep Sleep can fully manifest. Yogic sleep is withdrawing from outer reality but awakening to the inner light of Consciousness beyond all duality.

Radical Pratyahara, Yoga Nidra and Deep Sleep

The Yoga of Deep Sleep has a special relationship to pratyahara among the eight limbs of Yoga, requiring a yogic withdrawal of the prana, senses and mind. To enter into the ordinary state of deep sleep also requires Pratyahara or withdrawing from the senses, motor organs, outer prana and mind until we wake up the next day. The Yoga of deep sleep takes this process of pratyahara back further and more completely. It is not just an ordinary pratyahara or internalized state of mind; it is a radical pratyahara or complete withdrawal from body and mind, a kind of simulated death. This leads us to the state of nirodha or negation of the mind in Yoga practice.

Such radical pratyahara is another aspect of Yoga Nidra. In it we merge all of our pranic, sensory, motor and mental activities into the silent consciousness with the heart, the state of universal Self-awareness. This takes us to Cosmic Yoga Nidra in which we dissolve the entire universe into our own deeper consciousness. It is a simulated death to physical reality and opening to the formless realms of consciousness.

Another important aspect of the Yoga of Deep Sleep is cultivating peace and contentment in our daily lives, particularly the ability to surrender, relax and let go of all outer attachments, worries and concerns. This is the state of Lord Shiva who represents the supreme peace in which all is withdrawn and dissolved. Practicing pratyahara in the waking state helps us reach this Shiva state but that is just a preliminary aspect of it. Even when we are using the senses outwardly, we must learn to remain in this place of peace deep within. Then our waking state will link to the higher potentials of the deep sleep state as well.

Laya Yoga: Merging in Cosmic Sound and Light

The Yoga of Deep Sleep additionally relates to *Laya Yoga*, which is mergence of the mind into the Nada or sound current, the OM vibration and source of all mantras. That cosmic sound vibration lingers in deep sleep and supports it.

Laya Yoga as meditating upon this sound current or Nada is an important practice of Hatha Yoga and takes the practice of mantra to its highest seed state. As concentration of mind develops in meditation, an inner light and sound current naturally arises. Laya Yoga consists of merging into that current as a flow into transcendent awareness. It is often a simple approach of attentively listening to the nada and merging in the light, often identified with the deity or the guru. The sound current like music takes over the mind and draws it to higher levels of awareness.

Deep sleep is the laya or merged state of the individual being, where it returns to its core energies, impulses and aspirations. Turiya or the fourth state is when we are further merged into the universal and transcendent beyond our individual existence, which means that the hidden outgoing tendencies latent in the deep sleep state are removed.

Laya or the meditative state of mergence takes us to pralaya or the state of the Absolute when the universal creation is withdrawn, revealing the core of our being and of all existence beyond all qualities, energies and ideas. This transcendent state permeates the entire being with a sense of fullness, completion and perfection. This state is the Brahma Nirvana, or Nirvana of the Absolute mentioned in the *Bhagavad Gita*; this is the Turiya state. It is Yoga Nidra in the cosmic sense when the entire cosmic dream is withdrawn.

The Yoga of Transcendence and Turiya

The Yoga of Deep Sleep naturally leads us to the transcendent Yoga or "Yoga of the Fourth State", which ultimately consists of simply being the Self of all existence – the highest state of boundless Self-awareness without any limiting mental conditions. Having crossed over the darkness and ignorance of deep sleep, we enter into the boundless light and knowledge of our true nature. This Transcendent state is the basis and goal of all the Yogas of waking, dream and deep sleep, but it has its own quality and orientation as well. It can be experienced at any time of the day or night, and from various aspects and angles.

The transcendent reality though called the fourth state or Turiya is beyond all numerically defined states and conditions – the state of Oneness beyond all dualities and triplicities. It is sometimes divided further into several higher states, like Turiyatita or the fifth state beyond Turiya, or up to seven states. But these additional higher states are only aspects of Turiya or different degrees of immersion in it according to the simple older Upanishadic terminology. The *Upanishads* emphasize only four states.

This fourth state is only said to be transcendent relative to ordinary states of consciousness that are bound to the outer world of experience in body and mind. The transcendent state is in fact our natural state of unitary Self-awareness beyond all time and space, change and limitation. It is both immanent and transcendent, ever present and beyond all manifestation. It occurs naturally and effortlessly when we let go of identification with the external world and the thought-based mind.

We can call this transcendent state the nature of the Divine Self as the awakened cosmic dreamer. The Self that is the cosmic dreamer is not the self of the waking state, but the Self underlying waking, dream and deep sleep. Your true nature is not the Self of these three manifest states, but the background witness that can never be directly involved in the movement of time and is firmly rooted in eternity.

In the state of deep sleep, waking consciousness and the physical reality are withdrawn, and dream consciousness and the imaginative mind are also withdrawn. Prana continues in a withdrawn state along with the mind reduced to a seed state. Apart from that residual function of prana, we only know darkness, the void or ignorance. Yet underlying deep sleep the witness Self remains as the clear light of awareness through which we can enter into the fourth state.

The sense of I or Self is present continually in waking, dream and deep sleep, though projected outwardly. In the waking state, the "I am the physical body" predominates as our self-image and ego identity. In the dream state, the dream self is present along with the changing imaginations of the mind. In deep sleep, the Self is latent and has no objective reality as gross body or a subjective form as a dream body.

To reach the supreme Self we must cross over the three states of waking, dream and deep sleep, along with their inherent darkness, turbulence and misperceptions, without losing the continuity of our awareness – a formidable task indeed. We must put an end to the ignorance behind the state of deep sleep, the illusion in the dream state, and the apparent reality of the waking state, slaying the cosmic dragon. This is called crossing over the ocean of ignorance or Samsara, which is also a journey from darkness to light.

This transcendent state is the essence of all the other three states and sustains their higher qualities. It is the true wakefulness that never sleeps. It is our highest dream or aspiration. It is our deepest state of rest and relaxation. In it the mind is not necessary, though the mind can function outwardly as the occasion arises according to the necessities of karma. The Self is the state of pure existence beyond birth and death, coming and going. Spiritual awakening takes us into this ever wakeful state of Self-unfolding that has no end.

The ordinary person cannot cross over sleep or death to the other shore beyond the darkness of the mind, any more than an individual can swim across the ocean. Through the boat of knowledge, inquiry and the higher yogic teachings, the wise one alone can do so, but this requires determined effort, the most consummate striving, and the highest aspiration of the spirit connected to the full flow of grace from the higher light.

Your True Identity in Pure Consciousness

Whatever be the identity we assume in the outer world, we are bound to lose it over time, as the body itself is transient. Whether it is our identity relative to family, friends, work, country, religion or any other affiliation, such an identity cannot endure the relentless movement of time. *All outer identifications are misidentifications, projections of our self upon qualities, conditions, roles or appearances on the outside, just like our clothes and property. Like the latter, we must eventually let go of the former as well.*

The true Self endures the forms and expressions of our outer identity that change and fluctuate even over the course of a single day. The Self is continuous throughout the three states, but our identity changes radically along with them, from waking body, to dream imagination, to deep sleep darkness and all the diverse states of mind and prana in between.

The ego of the waking state disappears in dream, and our dream experience disappears in deep sleep. We get up in the morning and try to remember who we were before we fell asleep and what we were doing then, but forget what happened during sleep in between. In fact our identity is one of the greatest mysteries of our lives and about which we have the greatest ignorance. What we claim to be our true identity is just a passing outer phenomenon while our inner essence and true nature remains so unknown to us that we have even forgotten that its very existence. All of our outer identities are born of inner ignorance, sleep and darkness.

Our true identity is the Self within us, our nature as pure consciousness. That is all. We are who we are. We are as we are. We are not what we appear to be but who we are within, behind and beyond all appearances. Our inner identity is not how the body is constituted or how the mind thinks; it is the Self-nature of awareness that is pure light. Our true identity is not as a human person, or a physical body or even an intelligent mind. Our true identity is no separative identity at all; it is the presence of our inner being that is one with all. It has no name, form, gender, status, property, memory or expectations.

As long as we are identified with something bound by space and time, whether it is a body, emotion, idea or belief, our corresponding identity must be equally transient, unstable, limited and unreal. One's true Self is nothing that can be experienced or known by one's own mind or by the mind of another. The true Self has no image, quality, or action; and no external referent or effect. It is not subject to desire or fear, gain or loss, pleasure or pain, which are but the ups and downs of our outer experiences.

The true Self is the internal light and energy through which we can experience all our outer appearances in various lives and embodiments, but inherently transcends them. The Self cannot be known by science or any other collective means of knowledge and transcends all instruments and means of knowledge.

You can happily and freely lose your identity without losing your true Self. In fact, it is only by losing your outer identity that you can find your true Self – only by giving up any outer appearance, can you discover your enduring inner being and inner light. By forgetting your name and form, you can remember your true nature as pure consciousness and bliss.

Outer identity is a burden of past conditioning and outer expectations, something you are trying to create but can never sustain. It is a role that you take on for outer benefits, which may not be of any inner benefit at all. Your outer identity binds you to some external group or action that your connection with is only partial and tenuous. By giving up all identity we are free to be one with all, as that is our highest nature and potential. We are all and all is within us. Our bodies and minds are but the shadow of a deeper inner awareness.

Our waking identity has a certain continuity to it, affording it an illusion of stability, though it undergoes many changes and roles up to the time of our death. Dream experience allows us to create any number of identities out of our own imagination, and for any imagined period of time, but it is limited to the dream state and its rapid shifts and dissonances. Our identity in terms of name, age, vocation, location, beliefs, emotions or thoughts are all negotiable in the dream state. In dream we can even experience ourselves as another person, which we also do in the waking state watching movies or reading books. Clearly our identity is not fixed but always a work in process, yet one that can never be completed. Ultimately our identity eludes us and we must set aside what we thought we were or wanted to be.

Deep sleep shows us that we must lose our identity every night in order to renew our body and mind. To restore our ordinary outer identity once more for another day we must lose that identity in deep sleep every night. We have no identity in deep sleep, and no thought or action, but our being nevertheless endures. This experience reflects the inner wisdom that to find ourselves we must first lose ourselves—to gain lasting happiness we must first forget ourselves altogether.

The transcendent fourth state of pure consciousness shows us that we do not need any outer identity to be who we are. To be who we are we need only simply be, which is to be fully present in consciousness at every moment. We always remain identical with who we are, which is the highest light of awareness.

All outer identities represent a fall from consciousness, a projection of our awareness on to some external name, form, quality, action or association that is bound to limitation, karma, birth and death. What we are identified with confines our inner awareness. It is an external inertia that pulls our consciousness down, an unconscious and mechanical reaction that traps in mindless compulsions. It is a denial of our true Self to take up a circumscribed outer image as defining who we are. Mistaking the outer identity to be the self is like identifying oneself with one's shadow instead of with the one causing the shadow. Our external sense of identity has removed us from the reality of consciousness and made us into fragile commodities in the external world.

The transcendent Yoga requires that we become pure identity

without any identifications, pure Self-being without any Self-image, unitary being without any separate ego. This Yoga of transcendence takes us beyond all outer identity to an inner state of wholeness in which we are one with all and identical in essence to all that we see.

Pure Ananda or Universal Bliss

We experience some degree of happiness, joy or Ananda in waking, dream and deep sleep state. The allure of pleasure and enjoyment motivates our activity in the waking state. We similarly seek happiness in dreams, and even in deep sleep we are drawn into an inner state of contentment that is a type of ananda.

Yet all such external happiness experienced in waking and sleep is a reflected happiness that is transient in nature. It is mixed with sorrow and eventually comes to an end. Waking happiness is momentary and fleeting, limited by the duality of pleasure and pain in the senses. Dream happiness is imaginary and unreal.

Our most lasting happiness, and the least limited by outer circumstances, is the state of deep sleep, which is our natural root state of wellbeing. But even that is but a reflection of enduring happiness in the transcendent Sat-chit-ananda, Being-Consciousness-Bliss Absolute. Deep sleep is an unaware happiness that is not directly tangible, a happiness born of forgetting the stress and sorrow of our waking lives. Beyond it is the true Ananda as the Self, which is a positive overflowing of delight.

The Self is the source of all happiness, bliss, joy and Ananda. It is the basis of all rest, peace and rejuvenation. It is the eternal love of all existence as one's own. Whatever we love, we only love for its value to bring us to a state of oneness. We can only find peace and happiness within, not elsewhere. Yet eventually we also discover that everything dwells within us.

The Ananda of the transcendent state is conscious and unlimited, unlike the happiness of deep sleep. It is direct Ananda rooted in Being and Consciousness, not the reflected Ananda of the Anandamaya kosha in the deep sleep state. It is all pervasive like space and light.

The Singularity Beyond the Movements of the Mind

The *Yoga Sutras* refers to the Self-nature of the Seer as the goal of Yoga and the result of Samadhi,[29] but then states that otherwise, meaning apart from the Samadhi state, the Seer or Purusha assumes the nature of the vrittis or operations of the mind.[30] It is only at that point that the text begins the study of the functions of the mind. This indicates that that the functions of the mind dominate us only when we are not abiding in our true nature as the Seer.

The mind has five *vrittis* or functions according to the *Yoga Sutras*.[31]

1) Sleep as *nidra*, which includes deep sleep.

2) Imagination or *vikalpa*, which includes dream.

3) Memory or *smriti*, which is also present in dream.

4) *Pramana* or right knowledge, mainly in the waking state.

   Correct ascertainment of what is happening within and around us.

5) *Viparyaya* or wrong perception, mainly in the waking state.

   Incorrect ascertainment of what is happening within and around us.

These fluctuations in the mind, whether in waking, dream or deep sleep, are unstable, broken and often contradictory. Ultimately all the movements of the mind are forms of error and illusion, as the true reality, which is pure Being, is pure consciousness beyond the mind. Outer knowledge is a form of ignorance, a looking away from our true immortal nature to transient appearances. It is a knowledge of name, form and number that has ultimately no existential value and cannot change our consciousness.

Sensory perception can never reveal our true reality as the Seer. Reason can never discover the Self that is beyond all doubt. Even authoritative testimony cannot substitute for our own direct experience. Samadhi is the means of true knowledge that occurs only when we no longer take the movements of the mind as real or its knowledge as anything more than superficial. Turiya is the Samadhi state and is fully realized in Nirvikalpa Samadhi, in which we no longer identify ourselves with the mind and anything that it is capable of.

The Turiya state is referred to as the *akhanda vritti* or unbroken vritti, the unbroken state of awareness, said to be like a continual flow of oil, or the steadiness of a mirror. In one sense the transcendent state is no vritti or function of the mind at all. It is the *nirodha vritti* or the *nirvana vritti*, the negation of all the vrittis or outer actions of the mind. But it can be called a vritti or mode of awareness in the sense that it is the background of all the other vrittis and endures through them without losing its own nature. It is the deepest level of knowing, out of which all cognition or imagination arises.

The foundation of yogic meditation is to cultivate the *ekagra chitta* or the one-pointed vritti, which means to concentrate the mind and open up the Third Eye or unitary vision. When all other vrittis are absorbed into that single focus of attention it becomes akhanda or unbroken. It absorbs all other activities of the mind as all rivers flow into the sea. Yet we cannot fully focus our awareness on anything external. We must do so on our own Self and state of being, which is not bound by time and action.

This akhanda vritti is the *Atma vritti* or "mode of the Self", abiding in the I-thought that is the basis of all the other modes of the mind. The unitary unbroken mode of the Self, the flow of the pure I am, is the true cognitive state underlying all the multifarious broken modes of ego and mind.

This Atma vritti is also *Ananda vritti*. It has an inherent happiness and fullness, a lasting peace and bliss. It is also a *sphurana* or vibration, or like a wave but one that encompasses the entire ocean or vibratory field.

It is *Ananda lahari* or the "wave of bliss" that carries everything away and merges all things into the ocean of consciousness. We must learn to transform the state of deep sleep into that endless wave of bliss. That is the deepest level of Samadhi, in which Nirvikalpa Samadhi becomes Sahaja Samadhi or our natural state.

Yoga of Turiya or the Unitary Fourth State Continual State of the Witness - Turiyatita

The fourth or ever wakeful state is the yogic state of samadhi or unity consciousness that is the ultimate goal of Yoga. When we become fully established in it, no longer identified with the mind, we abide in the state of *Nirvikalpa Samadhi*, Samadhi without fluctuations, which is the state of Self-realization. Once we stabilize that throughout the day and at every moment, all bondage to karma comes to an end.

The practice underlying all the yogas of waking, dream and

deep sleep consists of cultivating the witness consciousness, detached from body and mind. To remain firmly in the witness state is to immediately cross over waking and sleep, time and space, birth and death. This begins with cultivating wakeful awareness throughout the entire day and night.

Cultivating the witness state is the core practice to reach the Fourth state of unity consciousness, but other support practices are also required. Remaining in that state continually even in the waking state is sometimes regarded as Turiyatita or the fifth state.

This transcendent Yoga rests upon two important background factors:

- First we should strictly follow a dharmic and conscious life-style, such as taught by the yamas and niyamas of Yoga practice. This includes a vegetarian diet, control of sense and motor organs, mind and emotions. Such a life-style is mandated for any deeper meditation practices.
- Second we must learn to sustain a moment-by-moment awareness. This entails regular meditation practices morning and evening, accompanied by mantra and other support practices, particularly a good power of attention, concentration and detached observation. But it must become inherent in our perception. This occurs when we learn to hold the mind at a contemplative level.

Jnana Yoga: Self-Inquiry
Asking the Question Who Am I?

The true Self that we are searching for is not the self of the waking state, but the Self underlying waking, dream and deep sleep. Normally we seek happiness for our physical wakeful self, which is but a dream and an illusion. True sadhana begins when we set the waking self and waking world aside as illusory, and learn to look within, uncovering the deeper veils of consciousness beyond the mind and senses.

This leads us to the practice of Self-inquiry, tracing the I-thought to its origins in the spiritual heart. One asks the question "Who am I?" and follows its examination deep within the heart and inner consciousness.[32] This I we are searching for is not the physical or psychological self that are already well known to us but the ground of consciousness hidden underneath them.

Most of us are not in a position to authentically ask the question "Who am I" as a spiritual quest. We may ask the question as to who we are but usually refer to our body, mind and memories.

To reach the place where we can authentically ask the question "Who am I?" is itself an important yogic achievement that rests upon first developing purity of body and mind, and release from our karmic debts to family, society, the world of nature, gurus and to the Divine forces underlying the universe.

Yet even more so, to authentically inquire into our true nature requires recognizing that we do not know who we really are; it also requires acknowledging that who we think we are is not truly so. It requires humility and a recognition of our deep-seated ignorance, which means recognizing the prevalence of the ignorance of the state of deep sleep in all that we do.

The main approach of Self-inquiry consists of asking "What is the Self underlying all three states of waking, dream and deep sleep?" This is not a mere verbal or rhetorical statement; it requires abidance in a state of inquiry and observation throughout day and night. Self-inquiry is not a mental game but a state of continual introspection. The question is not asked by the mind but is a questioning of everything that the mind does.

Self-inquiry has several stages from the outer to the inner aspects of our being.

1) First, one inquires into the nature of the pure I am beyond the identified or objectified self of the waking state or bodily self. Obviously the waking state is just one episode in greater life journey. The true Self is an inner reality, not an outer action or appearance in the material world.

2) Second, one looks into the nature of the pure I am beyond the self of the dream state, which holds hidden desires and wishes. The true Self is not a fantasy or imagination but a continuous awareness.

3) Finally, one looks to the pure I am beyond the Self of deep sleep, confronting the ignorance underlying our lives and recognizing our true identity as pure consciousness beyond. The true Self is not a state of ignorance or blankness but the pure light of consciousness.

When we ask the great question "Who am I?", what are we really asking? Who is the I that is asking the question? What is the *amness* or being of the I that we are looking into? What is the I or consciousness that is continuous throughout the fluctuations of the body and mind?

If we look carefully we can see that what we normally call the I, our bodily self, is not a real being. The I am the body idea or ego is a constantly changing construct or fabrication, put together by the shifting experiences of the mind. The continuity of the ego is broken by the states of dream and deep sleep. The ego itself is a kind of dream, caught unaware in the subconscious compulsions of instinct, sensation, emotion and conditioned thought responses. It is further broken by our shifting thoughts and emotions from moment to moment, with a space of consciousness underlying it that we seldom acknowledge.

Awakening to our true Self means dissolving our ego identity and the me and the mine. It requires recognizing that our inner Self is the Self within all beings and pervading the entire universe, the space of bliss that encompasses all in endless delight.

Mantra Yoga and the Fourth State

Energizing the entire OM vibration is a great aid in this process of moving into Turiya, the fourth state. OM is said to be the bow, our Self-awareness the arrow, and Brahman or the transcendent state the goal, as the *Upanishads* metaphorically state.[33]

The OM vibration is present in all the four states. It exists as a physical sound in the waking state, as a power of vision in dream, and as a power of mergence in deep sleep. In Turiya we merge into its inner silence beyond all vibratory changes, the supreme silence that is the basis of all Cosmic Sound.

Yet besides OM any important bija mantra can help take us to the Fourth State, if we merge it into its background silence. The bija Hrīm (Hreem) is particularly good for this, as it is the mantra of the spiritual heart (Hridaya). Or we can project a Divine name like OM Namah Shivaya! as the arrow of awareness directed to transcendence, the Shiva nature of pure awareness and peace. Beyond the three letters of OM as A, U and M, we experience the Nada, the vibration, and Bindu, the point focus underlying the mantra, in which the entire universe merges into the singularity of the inner Self.

All the great *Mahavakyas* or great sayings of Vedanta are relevant here like Aham Brahāsmi, "I am Brahman", and Sarvam Khalvidam Brahma, "Everything is Brahman". These powerful affirmations affirm our true nature beyond all the fluctuations of time. They reflect the wisdom of the fourth state.

Another related powerful mantra is OM Hrīm Hamsaḥ So'ham Svāhā, the mantra to the supreme light of consciousness (Paramjyoti), the supreme Shiva.[34] But it must be repeated with the light and sound of consciousness, not simply as a verbal pattern.

Bhakti Yoga of the Fourth State

Besides form based Bhakti Yoga, there is a formless Bhakti Yoga that works through direct surrender to the deity as one's true Self. This total surrender to the deity within the heart is the Ishvara Pranidhana of *Yoga Sutras* and prapatti of later devotional thought.[35] It can be aided by mantra or done directly as the highest attitude of devotion, aspiration and self-exceeding. One can merge into the Divine Self as the father, mother, brother, sister, beloved, guru, friend or master, as one wishes, but the concentration and consecration must be total.

Bhakti Yoga in the dream states provides access to the pure form realms of the deity, the Deva Lokas, but some duality remains. Bhakti Yoga in deep sleep allows us to merge into the deity as our background awareness, but a full sense of our identity with it is not yet present. Bhakti Yoga of the fourth state involves direct mergence into Ishvara as the lord and ruler of all but also as our inner controller and inner being.

We can cultivate Shiva as Parameshvara or the supreme Lord to arrive at this state, or any other deity orientation for that matter, whether Sri Krishna, Devi Sundari, Lord Hanuman, Ganesha, as we wish. It is the power of devotion that is the determinative factor. Pure unbroken devotion, beyond speech and mind, can take us to the Supreme as the Self of all.

In conclusion, whatever Yoga practices we perform resting in our true nature is a Yoga of the fourth state or Yoga of transcendence. This supreme Yoga can be practiced immediately and directly whenever we are ready to let go of the knot of mind and prana in our individual existence and merge into the boundless space of our own being.

Every day and each moment is an opportunity to return to our true nature that embraces the entire universe. OM Tat Sat!

Part IV

Exploring Deeper in Traditional Teachings

Mandukya Upanishad: The Secret of OM

The *Mandukya Upanishad* provides the clearest support for the Yoga of the Four States in the ancient Vedic teachings, and is the oldest text to expound it in detail. Yet this Upanishadic way of knowledge reflects an older teaching commonly taught in the *Vedas*, later expanded in yogic texts, and with a number of variations. Though the *Mandukya* is the shortest of the *Upanishads*, each verse is filled with deep meaning, like a set of axioms or Sutras.

Shankaracharya, the great Advaitic guru, explains this *Upanishad* and the four states in great detail in his commentary. In it, Shankara comments both on the venerable Upanishad itself and also on the *Mandukya Karika, a* brilliant commentary on it by his Paramguru, Gaudapada.

This *Mandukya Karika* of Gaudapada, along with Shankara's commentary, forms one of the foundation works of Advaita or non-dualistic Vedanta, unfolding the keys to the entire Yoga of Consciousness and Self-realization. Yet it is a very profound work that requires much deep study to approach. We would recommend every serious student of this Yoga of Consciousness to examine it slowly in a contemplative manner.

The following is my translation and short commentary on this important *Upanishad*.

Translation of *Mandukya Upanishad*

Section I.

1) OM. The imperishable syllable OM is everything. Now follows its explanation. What has been, what is and what will be, everything is only OM. And what is beyond these three periods of time, that is also only OM.

2) Everything is Brahman. The Self (Atman) is Brahman. This Self has four quarters.

Section II.

1) Dwelling in the waking state, with external knowledge, with seven divisions and nineteen channels, the enjoyer of what is gross, that is Vaishvanara, the universal person, the first quarter of OM.

2) Dwelling in the dream state, with inner knowledge, with seven divisions and nineteen channels, the enjoyer of what is subtle, that is Taijasa, the radiant, the second quarter of OM.

3) When while sleeping one has no desires, and sees no dream, that is deep sleep, Sushupti. In the state of deep sleep one's awareness becomes unified into a mass of knowledge. This is the state of happiness, with the enjoyer of happiness through the single channel of consciousness. This is Prajna, the power of wisdom, the third quarter of OM.

4) This deep sleep state is the lord of all, the knower of all, the inner controller, the basis of all, the origin and end of all beings.

5) Where there is no inner knowledge, no outer knowledge,

no inner and outer knowledge combined, no mass of knowledge, no presence of knowledge and no absence of knowledge. What is unseen, beyond all appearances, without mark, unthinkable, what cannot be taught, which is the essence of the perception of the unitary Self, beyond the manifest world, auspicious and non-dual, that the sages say is the fourth quarter of OM, that is the Self, that is to be known.

Section III.

1) One should know this Self as the imperishable syllable OM, by syllable, quarter, and measure, A-kara, U-kara, M-kara, the letters A, U and M.

2) The waking state and Vaishvanara is the letter-A, the first quarter, the first measure, as the origin it pervades all. One gains all desires and becomes foremost who knows this.

3) The state of dream and Taijasa is the letter-U, the second measure. Being elevated and holding both the other states of dream and deep sleep, one gains the continuity of knowledge and equanimity. No non-knower of Brahman is born in his family who knows this.

4) The state of deep sleep and Prajna, the letter-M, the third measure is the measure in which all things dissolve. One measures and dissolves the entire universe who knows this.

5) The measureless fourth state Turiya, beyond experience, the cessation of the phenomenal world, auspicious, and non-dual: That is OM; That is the Self. He enters by the Self into the Self who knows this!

Commentary on the *Mandukya Upanishad*

I) OM is the entire universe, comprising all time in its three states of past, present and future, and also what is beyond time. OM is our essential nature through the four states of waking, dream, deep sleep and Turiya, which constitute its four quarters. From it all time arises, including the movement of our lives through the past to the future, our prana and all of our karmas.

These four quarters of OM are the four aspects of our nature, symbolized by different forms of Agni as the flame of life and awareness, our inner soul or Self. We must learn to cultivate this ever-wakeful flame to understand our true nature and the nature of cosmic reality.

II) Vaishvanara here stands for the digestive fire as the root energy of the waking state, the individual soul in the waking state. His seven divisions are the seven subtle energies of Prana. The nineteen channels are the five sense organs, the five motor organs, the five tanmantras (sound, sight, touch, taste and smell), and the four aspects of the mind (ahamkara or ego, manas or mind, buddhi or intelligence, chitta or memory). In the Vedic view the digestive fire sustains the soul or Jivatman in the physical body and links us up to a higher intelligence within. It is not simply a biological phenomenon.

Taijasa stands for the radiant fire of the mind. It reflects memory, imagination and the essence of our waking experience that we have internalized. This subtle body has the same form and faculties as the physical body but is composed of energy rather than of matter and changes quickly according to our thoughts. The radiant mind lights up an inner vision and connects us with worlds of light and artistic vision. Prajna is the inner flame of wisdom that resides at the core of our minds hidden behind the veil of deep sleep. All happiness in life derives only from an ability to access the bliss or Ananda that is filtered to us through the restfulness of the state of deep sleep. The ability to withdraw into this inner state of mergence is the ultimate wisdom of life and the source of all transformative powers. Prajna connects us to the Divine presence and ruling power within us. That inner state of deep sleep is the seed and vortex underlying our entire outer manifestation through dream and waking. It connects us to the Divine power responsible for the universe.

The true Self is not an outer object that can be known through the mind. It is the unmanifest witness of all appearances and thoughts. It is beyond the three states of waking, dream and deep sleep, and can only be known through moving beyond them. It is the highest goal of life and the central support of all existence. It is beyond the known and the unknown as the supreme Knower and Seer of all. It is beyond all duality and inherently exists in tranquility, equanimity and serenity.

III) The four states of our daily consciousness correlate to the four aspects or letters of OM as A, U, M, and the silence beyond. OM is the vibration of cosmic consciousness that is the very sound of the Self arising from the transcendent space of awareness.

The waking state is the first state and holds the main experience of our embodied consciousness and the external world. The dream state partakes of both waking and deep sleep, as it has a form like the waking state but is internal like deep sleep. The deep sleep state absorbs everything back into itself.

Underlying these fluctuating states is the transcendent fourth, the state of pure unity beyond duality. It is the highest goal of knowledge, our true Self and flame of awareness within and underlying all these states. Realizing it is the essence of Upanishadic knowledge.

"The Self is Brahman", Ayam Ātmā Brahma, is one of the four *Mahavakyas* or Great Sayings of the *Upanishads*, used to directly point out the nature of Brahman as the Supreme Reality beyond time and space, birth and death. Each of the four *Vedas* has one such statement. This is said to belong to the *Atharva Veda*.

The Atman is one's innermost Self and essence of consciousness beyond body and mind. Brahman is the essence of Existence underlying the entire universe, form and formless. The statement that the Self is Brahman refers to the unity of the individual soul with the Absolute existence. It is amazing to think that the ancient sages could proclaim a realization of universal consciousness beyond time and space, at such an early era of human history. It was possible because of the Vedic science of consciousness, Self-inquiry and meditation that arose out of the mantras of the ancient Rishis.

Such statements of pure unity and nonduality are seldom highlighted in monotheistic traditions, which usually posit difference between the soul and God and the ultimate goal as heaven or paradise. They often interpret God as the creator apart from it, not as the underlying reality of the universe and beyond.

A number of mystics have similar statements to this Vedic declaration of cosmic unity, showing the universality of the teaching, but here the *Upanishad* provides a complete teaching and way of knowledge to go along with it. This Upanishadic teaching remains as relevant, fresh and powerful today, as when it was first composed several thousand years ago.

Chit-Shakti: the Power of Consciousness

Underlying our daily movement of consciousness is the supreme power of the universe, the Shakti of consciousness, Chit-Shakti. This inner power supports all the movements of our life from birth to death and beyond, and guides the changes in our awareness from waking to sleep and back to waking again. It supports nature's innate wisdom and the body's own intelligence down to a cellular level.

No one can stop the daily process of waking, dream and deep sleep. We may stay up late and postpone our sleep but we must eventually succumb to its irresistible force. There is an inner power at work that runs our lives; without it we are unable to even breathe or wink. This Chit-Shakti, the creative force arising from pure consciousness is close to us at all times and is our core energy. We must honor it fully as a spiritual force. We must not try to manipulate it merely for personal enjoyment.

Kundalini Shakti

This hidden power of consciousness holds secret potentials of transformation that we can cultivate through Yoga and meditation. It develops into the Kundalini Shakti, the inner yogic force or serpent power that arises from the base of the spine and draws us through unity consciousness to the highest awareness in the lotus of the head and beyond.

Crossing over the primordial ignorance of deep sleep to the light of pure consciousness rests upon Kundalini Shakti and is part of her awakening. The seven chakras mark different stages along the way of her awakening, unfolding subtle and causal, dream and deep sleep potentials from an individual to a cosmic level, to be eventually transcended into pure unity.

Kundalini Shakti is the power of cosmic sound, described as composed of the letters of the Sanskrit alphabet that represent how cosmic sound diversifies itself into the world of cosmic creation. Kundalini arises from the primal sound Pranava or OM that sustains all the vibratory forces of the universe and diversifies itself into the world of cosmic creation. Like OM, Kundalini has three and a half coils or aspects, which relate to the four states of waking, dream and deep sleep, and the hidden transcendent fourth beyond.

The OM vibration sets the Kundalini force in motion along with its tremendous energies that takes us beyond all time and space. OM is the basis of the four states of consciousness as we have noted. Yet OM is the basis of all other letters, sounds and mantras through which the diversification of creation occurs.

Kundalini Shakti relates to the four yogic levels of speech.

- Vaikhari or spoken speech, in the waking state, is seated in the throat of the physical body, and corresponds to the letter A of AUM.
- Madhyama or pranic speech, in the dream state, is seated in the heart of the subtle body, and corresponds to the letter U of AUM.
- Pashyanti or perceptive speech, in the deep sleep state, is seated in the navel of the causal body, and corresponds to the letter M of AUM.
- Para or the transcendent level of speech, in the state beyond mind and body, is seated in the root chakra, and corresponds to the Nada and Bindu beyond.

Awakened Kundalini arises from the Para state as the energy of Turiya or Transcendent awareness to move from the base of the spine to the top of the head and beyond. Vaikhari is the power of the waking state to articulate sounds with the vocal organs. Madhyama is the power of the dream state for the mind to project it imaginations and responses. Pashyanti is the power of deep sleep to connect us to seed sounds and vibrations. These are also the four levels of the OM vibration.

This power of consciousness exists beyond our entire biological existence, providing the energy and impetus for all life changes from birth to death. At death, it takes us to the subtle worlds and to an eventual rebirth. Developing it during life allows us to transcend death and rebirth.

Transitional Transformational Points in Awareness Doorways into Higher Perception

Transformational power points, or Shakti points, exist throughout, both in nature and within us, and can facilitate radical changes in awareness. We may use these Shakti points to facilitate higher changes in consciousness.

First are the Shakti points in daily time cycles like the junctures between waking and sleep at night and between sleep and waking in the morning. A similar such juncture point occurs between dream and deep sleep, though much harder to access. In the transition between waking and sleep we touch the light of the ever-wakeful Self. The same is true of the transition between sleep and waking in the morning.

This means that at the very moment we fall asleep, we have a doorway in consciousness to enter into the ever-wakeful state of the Self. We should learn to cultivate this moment, in which a spark of the Kundalini Shakti naturally comes forth.

We should prepare for sleep as a movement of transcendence beyond the waking self and its outer idea of reality. Then instead of simply falling asleep, we can move directly into deep meditation, consciously letting go of body and mind.

To be able to move into this state of conscious sleep, we should shut down all media and electronic influences at least two hours before sleep, so that the mind can empty itself out and return to its original pure nature. During this time, you can go out into nature for a few minutes and look at the night sky, or chant or silently meditate, or perform some rituals using ghee lamps or incense, or do whatever calms your mind. You must clear your mental field from the agitated patterns of the day; otherwise they will linger into sleep and carry their disturbances into the next day as well.

When you lay down to sleep, first voluntarily let go of your thoughts and hold to the inner light of awareness that is calm and self-contained. Shut the mind off and dwell in the space between your thoughts. Remind yourself that you are neither body nor mind, which are but your instruments, but the pure light of awareness. Your thoughts do not belong to you but are merely passing formations of the energies of the outer world, or the fluctuations in your outer body and mind, which your inner awareness is not affected by.

A mini-waking and sleep or birth and death happens along with all the different movements of our nature. This includes the opening and closing or winking of the eyes, and the movement of each breath with its inhalation and exhalation. Yogis know how to cultivate these points of transformation, as in the fixing of the gaze or holding of the breath.

Most importantly every sensory perception, particularly of natural phenomena, involves a waking awareness connected to the transcendent. The problem is that it only endures for the instant of perception, not for the time in which we think about the object. We must learn to prolong the instants of direct perception and link them together into a perpetual flow of lightning.

Special Junctures in Time

A transformative change occurs at all junctures (sandhis) between states of time in the world of nature, such as the sunrise between night and day or sunset between day and night. Other such important junctures are new and full Moons, solstices and equinoxes.

You can contact a doorway to the clear light of awareness at the special junctures of the day, such as sunrise, noon and sunset. The Gayatri mantra of Vishvamitra is specially used for this purpose, directing us not just to the light of the outer Sun but to the light of the inner Sun, the light of consciousness, beyond all the dualities of the outer world.

In the change of seasons, particularly from winter to spring and during the autumn season we can contact this inherent power of change in nature. Contemplating the seasons is part of accessing the eternal power of change beyond the seasons. We must learn to use the moments and movements of time to go beyond time to the eternal witnessing Self.

Different Levels of Days and Nights

The alteration of days and nights as periods of wakefulness and rest for the soul occurs at many levels. Day and night symbolize various states of activity and rest, light and darkness, expansion and contraction, manifestation and withdrawal – the very rhythms of our lives and of the universe overall. Each day and night is a self-contained dualistic movement.

Our entire physical life is a kind of prolonged waking state, with death as a prolonged dream and sleep until we awaken again in a new body.Our soul itself is a dream of the Divine.

In addition, the process of prana moving up the spine constitutes our inner day and the prana moving down the spine is our inner night. Some Yoga paths regard that conscious breathing can provide a full day, month or even year of spiritual evolution for the soul during each breath. Conscious breathing links us to the cosmic prana.

During the day our breath predominates in the right or solar nostril. During the night it predominates in the left or lunar nostril. The right and left or solar and lunar nadis, the Pingala and Ida, also represent the inner day and inner night of prana. The prana in the Pingala or solar nadi is the day and in the Ida or lunar nadi is the night.

Yet the alteration of days and nights or wakeful and restful periods occurs at every moment of perception. When the mind perceives something it is waking. When it rests and absorbs that perception it is its sleep state.

The highest sleep state or state of eternal rest is abidance in pure existence, Sat. The highest waking state is abidance in pure consciousness, Chit. The highest dream state is abiding in pure bliss, Ananda. Yet in essence all these three states are the same three facets of the infinite reality.

Brahma Muhurta

Brahma Muhurta, the period of two hours before sunrise, is the ideal time for meditation when the power of consciousness or Chit-Shakti is most naturally active. It is the ideal time of the day to connect with the forces of cosmic consciousness.

At Brahma Muhurta one can draw in the awareness underlying the deep sleep state into the waking state, energizing an inner wakefulness to our true nature. One can experience how the entire universe arises from Brahman as OM and cosmic sound vibration. At Brahma Muhurta we can move from deep sleep into Turiya merely through contemplating primal sound and connecting with the Nada or inner sound vibration.

We should awaken early each morning for our daily communion with the infinite. We can do this even while we are resting in bed. Once we have done this our day will proceed firmly rooted in the Divine, in an observant and creative state of awareness full of Shakti. We should experience daily life with a sense of the eternal, embracing the power of change as our own changeless nature.

Exploring Deeper Vedic Teachings

The Hindu Trinity

All creatures experience waking and sleep, not just human beings. These states are integral to the natural movement of life. We can easily observe the three states of waking, dream and deep sleep in animals. Ultimately, the entire universe follows the same states at a cosmic level as specific Divine powers. These levels of the deity also dwell within us.

The three states of waking, dream and deep sleep correspond at a cosmic level to the great trinity of Hindu deities as Brahma, Vishnu and Shiva as governing the cosmic processes of creation, maintenance and dissolution of the universe. They have their corresponding Shaktis or feminine powers of Sarasvati, Lakshmi and Kali. They relate to the three different aspects of the great cosmic mantra OM.

I. Cosmic Waking State

Lord Brahma

Lord Brahma is the creative principle among the Hindu trinity that rules over the cosmic waking state. He represents the awakening power of knowledge and cosmic law or dharma, seeding the spiritual teachings for all beings that arise from his contemplative energy. Brahma holds the cosmic power of speech, which is the dominant faculty in the waking state, and the main force of cosmic creation. This creative power relates to the cosmic power of rajas, the quality that sets everything in motion in the universe.

We should meditate in the waking state to remember and recognize its deeper reality at a cosmic level. This requires examining Lord Brahma's teaching through the *Vedas* and corresponding expressions of cosmic knowledge and the various sciences that are based upon it.

Ma Sarasvati

Lord Brahma's consort Sarasvati Devi reflects the same cosmic creative principle at a more artistic level. The waking state should not only involve factual or theoretical learning but also expression through literature, art, music, dance, painting, and sculpture. These creative endeavors help us understand how the forms and energies of the waking physical world arise and how they symbolize and convey higher realities. For this we should call upon Sarasvati's powers within us, her vibratory force of Divine action, communication and worship.

OM and the Cosmic Waking State

Lord Brahma, Devi Sarasvati, and the cosmic waking state relate to A-sound of the great mantra Aum.[36] The letter-A is the most basic sound from which all other sounds derive, the force behind all creation.[37] Waking is the A-vibration of OM that sets everything in the universe in motion, yet also reflects its unmanifest origin.

II. Cosmic Dream State

Lord Vishnu

Lord Vishnu as the sustaining power of the Hindu Trinity provides the inner energy to hold a harmonious level of manifestation, granting powers of protection, sustenance and fruition. Vishnu is the deity of luminous dreaming as the ruler of the higher mind or buddhi. When we connect to this Vishnu energy, we gain the power to bring inspiring dreams into the world and make them become real as beautiful and happy life experiences.

The most beautiful dream we can have is of life as a continual offering of devotion to the Divine, living according to a Divine purpose, identity and aspiration. Vishnu relates to the cosmic power of sattva guna, the energy that sustains and balances everything, allowing the manifest world to reflect the higher truth.

Ma Lakshmi

Lord Vishnu's consort is Ma Lakshmi, the Goddess of nourishment, abundance, beauty, wealth and delight, who blesses us with enduring sustenance at all levels of our lives. She fulfills our desires, dreams and wishes, both mundane and spiritual, letting the inner heart flower with devotion. Lakshmi indicates Divine love and devotion as a spiritual path, with everything we do as a heartfelt offering to the supreme.

OM and the Cosmic Dream State

Lord Vishnu and Ma Lakshmi and the cosmic dream state relate to the U-vibration of AUM.[38] The letter-U (oo) as a sound indicates vibratory energy, wave like motion, and a field of protected expansion and duration. This is the power of Vishnu and Lakshmi to hold our life energy at a deep level where it can sustain itself.

III. Cosmic Deep Sleep State

Lord Shiva

Lord Shiva represents the state of deep sleep as the place of mergence and unification. Shiva is the pure prana, the great unknown, and the supreme mystery underlying all things. Shiva governs over dissolution, which is not destruction but a return to the source.

In Hindu thought there is no real creation and destruction but simply the projection of the cosmic manifestation and its withdrawal back to its origin, like the rising and falling of waves on the sea or clouds in the sky. This force of cosmic deep sleep relates to the cosmic quality of tamas, cosmic entropy and inertia, the ultimate effect of time to bring all things to an end, driving everything towards both dissolution and transcendence.

Shakti, Ma Kali

Deep sleep relates to Shiva's consort as Ma Kali or the place of mergence, the dark Mother who withdraws all things back into her primal abode of pure potentiality. Kali is the power of time and karma that holds the seeds of all manifestation, but also the power of transcendence that draws us beyond form based expression to formless Being. Kali is the Yogi Shakti that draws all our energies and faculties within us for dissolution in our original consciousness. The demons that Kali slays represent illusory fears and desires born of the waking and dream states.

Deep sleep specifically relates to the Goddess Dhumavati, the elder form of Kali, who represents smoke, veiling and illusion. She is the grandmother spirit underlying all time. She is the great cloud of unknowing that puts everything to rest. She is Mula Prakriti or the root substance of the universe, and also the mystery that can take us beyond it.

OM and the Cosmic Deep Sleep State

Lord Shiva, Ma Kali, and the cosmic deep sleep relate to the

M-sound or *anusvara* vibration of OM, the background vibratory force from which all sounds arise. M itself is the sound of dissolution, pronounced with the closing of the lips and the drawing the sound inward and upward into silence.

AUM Pranayama

A	Waking state	Brahma, Creator, Rajas	Navel	Inhalation
U	Dream state	Vishnu, Sustainer, Sattva	Heart	Retention
M	Deep Sleep	Shiva, Dissolver, Tamas	Top of head	Exhalation

A special pranayama practice relates to these three deities and cosmic states. In this practice, called "AUM Pranayama", one gathers the breath in on inhalation, drawing it down to the navel below with the sound-A.[39] One holds the breath as retention in the heart, with the sound-U.[40] Finally, one lets the breath expand as exhalation through the top of the head with the sound-M.[41] The mind should follow the movement of breath in this process. This pranayama reflects the natural movement of transcendence through our daily states of consciousness that is reflected in every breath.

Every night as you go to sleep, follow this same movement of prana up the spine from the navel to the top of the head. Merge into the ascending AUM current, meditating upon the sound and meaning of this great mantra. Follow it beyond the mind into unbounded cosmic space, going beyond the darkness of sleep to the highest light of awareness. Experience all the Divine powers within you as aspects of your own Self and inner voice as OM!

You are Brahma, Vishnu and Shiva. You are Sarasvati, Lakshmi and Kali. Your waking, dream and deep sleep states reflect those of the entire universe.

The Vedic Cosmic Forms of the Four States

Individual Waking State	Vaishvanara	Cosmic Waking State	Viraj
Individual Dream State	Taijasa	Cosmic Dream State	Hiranyagarbha
Individual Deep Sleep State	Prajna	Cosmic Deep Sleep State	Ishvara
Individual Turiya	Atman	Cosmic Turiya	Brahman

There is another ancient formulation of the cosmic side of the four states that the *Upanishads* speak of at an individual level. These four aspects of the universal Self reflect a cosmic level of consciousness like Brahma, Vishnu and Shiva but in a different way.

Viraj, the Vedic deity of the cosmic waking state, means splendor and refers to the collective or universal physical Self, corresponding to Vaishvanara at an individual level. To experience Viraj is to experience the entire physical universe as oneself, with your eyes and ears, hands and legs everywhere and all physical forces, creatures and worlds as your own manifestations.

Hiranyagarbha is the collective or universal subtle or dream self, corresponding to Taijasa at an individual level. Hiranyagarbha means the golden seed or fetus and is sometimes identified with the Cosmic Prana, as the creative energy underlying the universe. To experience Hiranyagarbha is to experience the entire astral or dream cosmos within oneself, with all its play of light, radiance, beauty and art.

Hiranyagarbha has another meaning as the name of the original teacher of the Yoga Darshana of the six Vedic philosophies, out of which the Patanjali *Yoga Sutras* later arose as the prime text. Hiranyagarbha is sometimes regarded as a human teacher, other times as a cosmic principle. Yet sometimes Hiranyagarbha is another name for Ishvara described next. As such Hiranyagarbha is another name for the solar Godhead in the Vedas.

Ishvara is the universal aspect of the causal Self, corresponding to Prajna at an individual level. Yet Ishvara is also a general term for the Divine consciousness operating the universe as its master force, sometimes identified with Paramatman, the Supreme Self.

Unlike the individual soul, Ishvara is not qualified by ignorance or Avidya or the state of deep sleep, but is the Lord of Maya and all the movements of time. As such, Ishvara is the original guru of Yoga mentioned in the *Yoga Sutras*. To experience Ishvara is to be one with the supreme Lord, whose manifestation is the entire universe, gross, subtle and causal. Ishvara, in masculine or feminine forms, is the prime deity of devotional approaches, or Bhakti Yoga.

Understanding these three aspects of the cosmic Divine in the three states takes us to the realization of Brahman or the supreme reality beyond all manifestation, the transcendent fourth. Ishvara, Hiranyagarbha and Viraj are the three aspects of Brahman, the transcendent reality and correspond to Prajna, Taijasa and Vaishvanara. The Atman, Purusha or Self is the fourth transcendent reality.

Great Yogis can enter into the samadhis of these four cosmic aspects, experiencing the entire physical universe as their Viraj form; the entire subtle universe as their Hiranyagarbha form; and the entire causal universal as their Ishvara form; ultimately extending to the formless Brahman beyond as the fourth state.

At a supracosmic level, the manifest universe is sometimes said to be the waking state of the deity and the unmanifest realm beyond as its sleep. Yet more commonly, the manifest universe is said to be the dream of the cosmic being, when it imagines other worlds and creatures. The unmanifest state is its waking reality, when it is aware of its own nature.

Agni Vidya of the *Vedas*, the Inner Flame of Awareness

The Vedas begin with the worship of Agni,[42] the inner sacred flame that sustains our own light of awareness, the Divine Self within the heart, such as taught later in the *Mandukya Upanishad*. The Vedic terminology, though using some of the same terms as later texts, is a little different than that of the *Upanishads*. Vedic expression reflects an earlier symbolic-poetic period of human thought, prior to the ascendency of reason and abstract thought. This Vedic Agni is the flame of consciousness, wakefulness, attentiveness and mindfulness. It is the basis of all the four states, particularly at an individual level, but sometimes at a cosmic level as well.[43]

- In the *Rigveda*, long before the Upanishadic era, *Vaishvanara*, which means the universal person, is said to be Agni's cosmic or heavenly form as the Sun or Paramatman, the supreme light, representing the liberated soul.
- *Jatavedas*, which means the knower of all births, is his atmospheric form as the individual soul or power of rebirth and regeneration.

- *Agni* as a specific term is his earthly form in the outer world, including the material or elemental fire.
- We can identify this Agni form with the waking state, Jatavedas with dream, and Vaishvanara (like Ishvara) with deep sleep.

The real Vedic fire offering consists of enkindling the flame of awareness within us and sustaining it throughout all states of waking, dream and deep sleep, birth and death, transcendence and immortality. This is the ongoing fire offering of moment-by-moment consciousness and forms the Vedic practice of Self-inquiry. We can also practice it through the breath by offering each breath into the inner fire of Prana in the heart.

The Vedic Yoga directs us to offer all our thoughts into the inner fire of awareness, which is the highest inner sacrifice or Yajna.[44] Then all that we do will be purified and turned into the light of truth. We must search back within our minds and hearts for the immortal fire of the Self at the core of our being. This search for this inner flame can be approached from various angles, as it is the essence of feeling, knowing, volition and perception. It is sometimes likened to a search in a secret cave, the cavity of the heart.

Vedic Solar Yoga and the Mystic Sun

The cosmic form of Agni is *Surya* or the Sun, which symbolizes the Self as the universal light of truth. This is the inner Sun of unbounded consciousness, not the Sun as a mere outer light form.[45] The Vedic Fire Yoga extends to an expanded Vedic Solar Yoga as the pursuit of enlightenment and Self-realization. According to this teaching, your true Self is the inner Sun, the light of lights, the Self of the universe, hidden in the darkness of ignorance. We must awaken, release and unfold that Divine light within us.

The *Chandogya Upanishad* speaks of the various forms of the rising and setting of the Sun, taking us eventually to a perpetual day when the Sun neither rises, nor sets.[46] This symbolizes the unitary state of Self-realization beyond the dualities of mind and prana, waking and sleep.

The *Vedas*, like many ancient mystical teachings, including those of ancient Egypt, speak of the resurrection of the Sun out of darkness. This is the inner mystic Sun of Divine awareness trapped in the darkness of mortality and the movement of time through the days and nights, births and deaths of the soul. This solar teaching also includes experiencing the night Sun, the secret light of consciousness illuminating the darkness of deep sleep.

Bringing back this inner Sun requires crossing over the night of ignorance. Crossing over the night means maintaining the light of consciousness over the darkness of deep sleep. This means taking the Sun, which represents our daily awareness through prana and mind, out of the cycle of time to a perpetual day of pure awareness. This may involve the image of crossing over the night in a sun boat or boat of awareness.

The Vedic Gayatri mantra is the most important and commonly used Vedic verse. It is chanted daily, at the rising of the Sun, noon and the setting of the Sun. Gayatri is a prayer to reach the highest light, to Savita, the transformative aspect of solar energy, and the inner power of Yoga.

> We meditate upon the supreme light of the solar transformative deity; may he guide our intelligence.
> Rigveda III.62.10

The Gayatri mantra takes us beyond the darkness of the world of duality to the immutable light of the inner solar Self. It aids us through all transformation as we awaken to ever higher levels of consciousness.

OM, Lord Shiva and the Four States

Among the Hindu deities, Lord Shiva is most specifically identified with OM and said to be Omkara itself. Shiva is the deity of the state of dissolution at a cosmic level and deep sleep, the M-vibration of AUM. Deep sleep is the state of Shiva. Shiva is the state of rest to which all things return. As such Shiva is a deity of the deep sleep state as pure peace. Yet Shiva is also the deity of pure Being, Sat, the immutable existence into which all things merge.

In this regard, Shiva is the deity of the supreme dissolution in the fourth Transcendent state or Turiya. Shiva is the source of all mantras and of the Sanskrit alphabet that arises from the beating of his drum, as the original cosmic sound vibration.[47]

OM Namaḥ Śivāya! is an important mantra to keep us awake in the deep sleep state and connect us to Turiya, or with its special bijas OM Haum Jūm Saḥ Namaḥ Śivāya![48]

The Tryambakam or Mrityunjaya mantra (Rigveda VII.59.12) is for taking us over death, which also means the darkness of duality that keeps us bound to the cycle of time and under the ignorance of deep sleep.[49]

Krishna and the Mystic Night

Krishna as a word refers to that which is dark, black or dark blue in color and energy, mystery and intoxication. In this regard, Lord Krishna is the deity of the mystic night of bliss and Divine Love, the great night of unknowing that allows us to cast away all ignorance and sorrow into eternal happiness and rest. This mystic night does not refer to the darkness of ignorance and deep sleep, but to the power of bliss or Ananda to absorb all things back into itself, the transcendent fourth state. This is the darkness, like the dark pupil of the eye, which holds the power of perception. Krishna's play or lila and his dances and meetings with his consort Radha occur on this mystic night of Ananda, which is also an extension of deep sleep into the Turiya state.

When we awaken in deep sleep, the Anandamaya Kosha or bliss sheath is merged into pure Ananda. We do not simply feel the contentment of sleep but that of universal peace and Divine love filtered down to us.

The deep sleep state has a magnetic quality, a gravitational force to draw all things back into it and merge them within it. Krishna represents this Divine power of attraction that draws us through and beyond ignorance and sorrows with the irresistible power of devotion. This magnetic power can be contacted by the seed mantras *Klim (Kleem)* that is the Shakti of love and Ananda.

Exploring Deeper Yogic Teachings

The *Yoga Sutras* defines Yoga as samadhi, teaching a Yoga of samadhi as its foundation Yoga. Developing samadhi requires transforming the natural unconscious samadhi of deep sleep into higher conscious samadhis. The highest samadhi of Self-awareness, also called the Sahaja or natural state of awareness, is the essence of the Turiya or transcendent state. Beyond the rest of sleep is the unbounded peace of your own true nature as the Purusha or seer of all.

Samadhi can be correlated with yogic sleep or Yoga Nidra in the higher sense of the term, a negation of all the fluctuations of the mind, and a mergence into the state the Seer, in which the mind and all phenomena become dissolved and are transcended. The ultimate Yoga Nidra is Being-Consciousness-Bliss absolute beyond all manifestation, in which all the universes are dissolved.

The eight limbs of Yoga can be viewed as aspects of samadhi, which is their culmination or highest state. All eight limbs of Yoga involve various degrees and levels of creating peace, calm and stillness in the different aspects of our nature, right from the body to our highest intelligence, a samadhi-like calming effect.

The first two limbs of Yoga, Yamas and Niyamas, are rules and attitudes of right living that help calm the body and mind, removing turbulence, inertia and agitation from our minds, behavior and action.

Relative to the five Yamas, Ahimsa or the attitude of non-violence removes agitation from the mind and emotions, which are often dominated by envy, jealousy, anger and conflict. Satya or truthfulness makes the mind steady and allows us to contact the deeper truth within us. Brahmacharya or control of creative energy turns all our energies within and allies them with the cosmic creative force. Asteya or non-stealing helps us let go of attachments, realizing that nothing in the outer world belongs to us. Non-coveting or Aparigraha, which also indicates non-clinging or holding on to anything, helps us release any mental fixation on the material world.

Relative to the five Niyamas, one of the best forms of Tapas is sustaining a wakeful awareness through mantra and meditation, cultivating the inner flame of awareness. Svadhyaya, self-study, involves examining our own consciousness throughout the day and implies ongoing introspection. Ishvara Pranidhana implies surrender to the ruling consciousness underlying the state of deep sleep within us, also called Ishvara. Saucha or purity removes toxins and distortions, including the impurities of the mind that arise from attachment to the material world. Santosha promotes the contentment of inner rest and relaxation, the Ananda that pervades deep sleep.

The Yamas and Niyamas form the *adhikaras* or prerequisites, the right frame of mind and proper life-style, necessary for deeper meditation to flower. Yet each of the Yamas and Niyamas is like a different name and definition for Yoga overall and is relevant for all Yoga practice. They form the foundation so that the six practice limbs of Yoga that follow them occur from a level of higher awareness, rather than as merely actions arising from body consciousness.

Asana stills the body, much like the stillness of the body that arises naturally in the sleep state, but aiming at a sitting pose that holds a higher awareness and wakefulness. Later one may develop that stillness while laying down as well.

Deep Pranayama places us into a simulated deep sleep, in which a higher prana purifies the mind and brain. It removes the breath from its fixation on outer reality to deep composure and repose. Pranayama implies moving the prana within, creating a unitary prana, in which all the other pranas are calmed and absorbed. This is what happens when we sleep. In sleep, particularly deep sleep, a deeper prana prevails and sustains body and mind.

Pratyahara reflects the withdrawal of the senses that occurs naturally in sleep. Pratyahara is in fact a state of simulated sleep. Maintaining a continual awareness in sleep includes a natural deep Pratyahara, extending far beyond what one can do in the waking state. Learning to turn the senses off, which requires learning to withdraw our attention from the senses at will, is one of the keys to deep meditation.

Dharana means developing a state of concentration or continual awareness, as detached from the physical body and the outer mind. Being able to observe the ignorance of the mind in waking and sleep allows a powerful concentration to occur.

Dhyana is meditation and holds the mind in a steady reflective state much like the formless mass of consciousness in deep sleep. Meditation requires moving into our inmost consciousness, dissolving the mind in stillness.

Samadhi is full mergence in conscious rest or sleep, remaining awake in our inner being and detached from the outer changes of waking, dream and deep sleep. The highest Samadhi consists of total immersion in the light of consciousness in which the external world becomes but a shadow.

OM and the *Yoga Sutras*

Patanjali teaches that the best way to reach Samadhi is Ishvara

Pranidhana or surrender to Ishvara, the ruling Divine power that dwells within us and within the universe as a whole, the Adi Guru or original teacher of Yoga.[50] Patanjali propounds that the indicator or voice of Ishvara is Pranava, the primordial sound vibration that is OM.[51]

OM is power of Ishvara, the Adi guru of Yoga in the *Yoga Sutras.* This emphasis on repeating and meditating on OM in the *Yoga Sutras* suggests the entire Yoga of OM as taught in the Upanishads that Patanjali likely knew.[52] Patanjali's *Yoga Sutras* as a Vedic philosophy implies acceptance of the authority of the Vedic teachings and his text employs Vedic terminology starting with the Purusha as the inner Seer, and rooting the teaching in OM.

Patanjali prescribes meditation on Pranava or OM, including its meaning. This naturally implies the connection of OM with the four states of waking, dream, deep sleep and Turiya as in the Upanishads. OM in its full vibration holds the Transcendent state merging into silence, primordial sound resting in its own nature.

Attitudinal and Perceptual Changes of Raja Yoga

Hatha Yoga emphasizes psychophysical techniques involving body, prana and senses, moving and directing them in various ways to bring about changes in our consciousness. Raja Yoga emphasizes what can be called "attitudinal and perceptual changes" that can be done directly.

Asana holds the body in a certain posture so we can experience physical reality in a different way. Pranayama helps us redirect our Prana to a higher awareness. Such external changes are easy to make, yet they remain limited if we do not take them farther.

Attitudinal changes reflect the levels of Dharana and Dhyana, concentration and meditation. They ask us to change our attitudes in life, like replacing hate with love, or anger with compassion. This is the *pratipaksha bhavana* or meditation on opposite qualities of the *Yoga Sutras*.[53] Perceptual changes ask us to change how we view ourselves and how we view the world. This includes practices like learning to be aware of the space between objects or the gap between thoughts, or how to focus our vision into a single point of concentration. These are methods of Raja Yoga. Yet beyond these are the changes in consciousness born of Self-inquiry in which we no longer identify with either body or mind.

Attitudinal and perceptual changes can be brought to the level of the Purusha or inner Self, by affirming and contacting its transcendent nature. The Purusha as beyond the body and mind can easily let go of any condition of body and mind that it wishes to detach from. All physical and mental difficulties and limitations have nothing to do with you in your true nature as pure consciousness, any more than the moon is afflicted by its distorted reflection in a wind blown lake. If you affirm your Purusha nature, you may change anything in yourself that needs to be changed, as you will no longer be attached to any movements of the mind.

The Yoga of Consciousness through the four states is primarily a Raja Yoga or higher Yoga of meditation. It rests upon a number of important attitudinal and perceptual changes. A few such typical awareness changes are indicated below.

Attitudinal Changes

- To recognize that the waking state is only one-quarter of our greater existence; not the whole of it nor its essence.

- To recognize that our physical life is a dream of our immortal unbounded soul; not its true realm of existence.
- To recognize that the mind is largely a conditioned intelligence caught in ignorance; not a conscious awareness but a karmic reaction system.
- To recognize that pride and arrogance is a sign of an undeveloped mind. Thinking that we already know is the greatest obstacle to true knowledge.
- Not to bow down to petty emotions, desires, fears and attachments of the waking state. Emotions do not belong to you but are reactions of the outer body and mind.
- To hold to what is eternal and let go of what is transient, recognizing the impermanence inherent in all of our experiences, including our waking reality, physical body and outer personality.

Perceptual Changes

- To see the body as an instrument of expression in the outer physical world; not as our true Self.
- To regard our motor organs as instruments of outer action; not our true being.
- To regard our sense organs as instruments of gaining sensory impressions; not our inner power of perception and discernment.
- To see the mind as an instrument of experience and expression in the realm of ideas; not as our true Self.
- To see the world as an appearance of a deeper reality beyond time and space; not as real in itself. To inquire

into the reality underneath all appearances.

- To see the ego as a confusion of subject and object and our true Self as beyond all images and identities. The true Self has no image or identity and is of the nature of pure light.
- To regard the true Self as the witness, not any fluctuation of body, prana or mind or any observable quality.
- To reject all external objects as unreal apart from the Self.
- To reject all thoughts and movements of the mind as external to the Self.
- To see the Self in all beings and all beings in the Self like images in a mirror.

Moving from the Outer Mind to the Inner Mind

The Yoga of Consciousness requires that we move from the outer mind, which is the seat of our normal awareness, to the inner mind, which is the seat of contemplation and meditation, and from that to the inner consciousness beyond the mind. This is a step-by-step process.

The outer mind is where consciousness resides when we are dealing with the material world and outer human personality, our waking and physical reality and individual ego. This is the main domain of conscious awareness for the normal human being. Yet it is an awareness largely devoid of any inner consciousness, Self-awareness, Self-consciousness or capacity for introspection.

The inner mind only comes into play when we learn to practice Self-inquiry and meditation. In Self-inquiry we learn to question who we are and what the world is. We search out for ourselves the fundamental questions of life at a perceptual and experiential level. In meditation we learn to observe and silence the mind.

Dwelling in the inner mind means that we learn to question the outer mind, question who we think we are and what we regard as the nature of reality. We learn to use the senses in a contemplative manner, rather than as mere instruments of enjoyment. We create a conscious stream of introspection and Self-inquiry in the mind to counter habitual thought patterns.

While the outer mind reflects the external world of the senses, the inner mind reflects the inner realm of consciousness beyond body and mind. The inner mind gradually merges into the inner consciousness and its separative existence disappears. Through it the mind on both inner and outer levels becomes an instrument of a deeper Self-awareness. Then the mind becomes an instrument of expressing or teaching the nature of Self-existence.

The Yoga of the Four States and Buddhism

Buddhism, like Hinduism, uses the great mantra OM, but with a slightly different meaning, identifying OM with Shunyata or the Void. OM is part of many Buddhist mantras like OM Ah Hum. In the Buddhist philosophical system of Yogachara or the eight consciousness system, there are eight factors of awareness as the five senses, manas (outer mind or manas), vijnana (inner mind or buddhi) and the Alaya Vijnana or the storehouse consciousness.

The storehouse consciousness can be identified as Avidya and the state of deep sleep. Beyond the Alaya or deep within it dwells the Tathagata Garbha or seed of Buddhahood, which connects us to the transcendent state. This is also the

Bodhichitta or enlightened mind that dwells within the heart. In Buddhist thought Bodhichitta or Prajna or the pure mind or self-natured awareness serve a similar role to define consciousness.

The Great Gurus

The great gurus who achieve Self-realization never die. They dwell in the true Self that exists behind and beyond all states of consciousness bound by time. Crossing over the darkness of ignorance of deep sleep they enter into the eternal timeless reality that encompasses all time on every side. They transcend waking, dream and deep sleep in the ever-wakeful fourth state. For them, death is nothing, just a falling off of external veils. They have long gone beyond the illusion of physical reality.

As pure consciousness, neither birth nor death can ever apply to them. They have long departed from body consciousness and identification with the individualized mind, nor do they take the external world as real. They dwell in the ever consciousness state and witness the dream of physical reality when alive. After death they remain in the same eternal state but no longer witness the bodily dream.

There is no need to mourn for the death of such great masters because they remain in their own unlimited state of awareness, both during life and after death. There is nothing lost for them in dying and nothing gained in being born. Their intelligence has transcended the ignorance and ego of the mind. They do not need a mind or a body to be happy or to be aware. They are not concerned about any recognition, heritage or remembrance in the illusory waking world.

For the great gurus there is only an unending day of continual awareness that encompasses all days, whether past, present or future, including the lives of all creatures, worlds and universal manifestations. From the inner point of unitary awareness they can grasp the periphery of all possible existences in time and space, in all worlds and in all creatures.

Bhagavan Ramana Maharshi

Bhagavan Ramana Maharshi was an extraordinary guru who had mastered the Yoga of Consciousness and the Four States from the young age of sixteen. This was not a matter of any formal practice but of his own spontaneous meditation practice. Ramana always asked his students and visitors about their sleep, whether they slept well, and how they experienced the state of deep sleep and how they felt about it. In this regard, he was not worried about their sleep patterns in terms of physical health. He was inquiring as to whether they were able to maintain their inner consciousness throughout the sleep state and contact the inner Self behind it. He was actively teaching the Turiya Yoga or Yoga of the Fourth State, suggesting them to maintain Self-remembrance even in deep sleep.

Ramana lived in the natural state of pure consciousness merged into the spiritual heart beyond the mind. His presence was the primary teaching. His teachings provide tremendous insights on how deep sleep and the transcendent state are connected can be linked, continuous moment-by-moment awareness by day and by night. The Self does not disappear in deep sleep and by remembering that state we can connect to it while waking. We can live in the state of Self-realization.

****

Closing Points and Practices

Below are a few closing comments to sum up this teaching on the Yoga of Consciousness and important points of convergence.

Daily assessment of your Yoga practice

Most of us examine our Yoga practice over time, noting how it has developed or progressed, generally on a monthly or yearly basis. We must learn to do this every day. Every day is a different life for the soul. Every day is a new life, a new experience and a new practice that should be carefully regarded. Remember to perform your daily yogic Self-reckoning and Self-remembrance.

Keeping track of your dreams

It is important to keep track of your dreams, writing them down in a journal if we need to, particularly dreams that are inspiring or evocative. In this way we can learn to map out our dream life, dream landscape and hidden dream potentials, noting our inspirations and fears in the dream state.

We should learn to understand the particularities of our dream self and dream world, just as we note those of the physical world. Our dream realm, though much more variable than the waking world, does have some degree of continuity and particular areas of repeated focus. Yet we should remember at the same time the illusory nature of the dream state.

Holding to the same thought on sleep and waking

Another practice to sustain consciousness through sleep is to hold a single thought, particularly in the form of a mantra, from waking into dream and deep sleep, trying to awaken with that same thought or mantra in your mind in the morning. Once the mind is ruled by a single thought it can more easily hold a unified awareness. Best is to use a mantra, especially a bija mantra like OM or Hrīm (Hreem) for this purposes, or to repeat some Divine name or extended mantra like Gayatri mantra.

Contacting the Light of the Heart

Another method is to merge into the light of the spiritual heart (hridaya) as the origin of waking, dream and deep sleep. That is the light of higher wisdom and compassion. For this practice, we simply hold a background attention in the spiritual heart, concentrate on it as the core of our being and view our changing states of waking, dream and deep sleep as peripheral states moving around it. We can merge the mind into the heart, or we can keep our awareness rooted in the heart throughout the day.[54]

Understanding Ignorance as Deep Sleep

Deep sleep is only dark because we are attached to the reality of the waking state. As we turn within, deep sleep becomes full of light. The degree of unconsciousness that we experience during deep sleep equals our attention on the external world during waking state. As we bring more awareness into the waking state, so we bring more light into the state of deep sleep. The state of peaceful unitary Self-awareness has an even greater power of renewal than the state of deep sleep. We must aim to cross over the ignorance of our true Self in the state of deep sleep and discover our true Self as the light of eternal awareness.

Conclusion

This great Yoga of OM and its relationship to the four states of waking, dream, deep sleep, and Turiya, is one of the most important teachings in all of Yoga since Vedic times. It is one of the simplest and most powerful Yoga practices that is relevant to everyone. It takes us beyond outer divisions and practices of Yoga and makes our entire daily life, including sleep, into a powerful Yoga practice and way of meditation.

Such a comprehensive Yoga approach cannot be reduced to a few techniques or en masse practices, though these can be part of. It requires understanding our own unique daily life as a natural movement of higher consciousness. In closing, what follows are a few suggestions about its application.

Learn to transform your daily activity into a daily adventure in consciousness. Observe the changes of waking, dream and deep sleep with profound attention, as containing many secret doors to higher awareness. This is ultimately much more fascinating and engaging than any form of entertainment or study.

Cultivate a moment-by-moment awareness so that you are always alert and responsive. Let everything that comes into your consciousness function as a reminder to become more aware of your inner being. Remember your eternal pilgrimage in consciousness and that each day is a stage in its cosmic unfoldment.

Be aware of how your daily movements from waking to dream and deep sleep affect your body, prana and mind. Remain awake within your eternally wakeful Self. Remember that to fall asleep in consciousness or to lose our awareness is the greatest calamity. Do not be heedless, thoughtless, distracted or disturbed. Sustain the highest composure.

Value every day as the ultimate day, the eternal day of your eternal Divine Life in the Divine Light of consciousness. Try to bring out your eternal potential every day in a new way. One way to do this is to view each day as the last day of your physical life; a life that you should use as a path beyond time and death. Another way is to view each day as the first day of your new life of spiritual awareness, letting go of all negative experiences from the past.

Yet another way is to attune yourself to the power of consciousness that moves you through the three states like an electrical current. Hold to that power that links all levels of your life and mind. Let it take you beyond the mind as well. Your consciousness is the inner guide of the drama of your life. Its power is the basis of all other powers. Honor that supreme Shakti of awareness.

Remember that your inner being and true Self is the central still point of consciousness around which all the movements of body and mind revolve, yet is not affected by them. Learn to be that true Self that is all-pervasive and finds bliss and light everywhere!

Part V

Appendices

1. Sanskrit Glossary

Agni – fire and light as cosmic principle

Ahamkara – ego or self-identification as a function of the mind

Ananda – bliss or state of fullness

Antahkarana – mind as inner instrument

Apana – downward moving Prana

Atman – Self, Self-nature

Ayurveda – traditional Vedic system of mind-body medicine

Bhakti Yoga – Yoga of Devotion

Bindu – primal energy points

Brahma – Creative force of Hindu trinity

Brahman – absolute or transcendent reality

Buddhi – higher discriminating power of the mind

Chakra – energy center in subtle body

Chit – pure consciousness

Chitta – mental field or field of conditioned consciousness

Devata – Divine or cosmic power or principle

Dharana – concentration as a Yoga practice

Dhyana – mediation as a Yoga practice

Dosha – Ayurvedic constitutional quality, biological humor

Guna – prime quality

Hatha Yoga – Yoga of psychophysical techniques and prana

Havan – Fire offering

Ishvara – Cosmic lord or ruling power, original guru of Yoga

Jagrata – waking state

Jnana Yoga – Yoga of knowledge

Kaivalya – natural state of the Self beyond the gunas

Kali – Goddess of time and transformation

Kapha – biological water humor or dosha in Ayurveda

Karma Yoga – Yoga of right living, service and ritual

Kosha – sheaths of the inner being or Atman

Krishna – the avatar of Yoga

Lakshmi – Goddess of devotion

Laya Yoga – Yoga of mergence in the sound current

Manas – mind, specifically outer sensory aspect

Mantra – energized speech and sound

Maya – illusion of outer appearances

Nada – cosmic sound vibration

Nidra – sleep

Nirodha – completely controlled state of mind, consciousness disidentified from its mental instrument

Ojas – essence of vitality

Patanjali – compiler of *Yoga Sutras*

Pitta – biological fire humor or dosha in Ayurveda

Prakriti – Nature or the observable

Pramana – means of right knowledge

Prana – life force both individual and cosmic

Pranava – primordial sound

Pratyahara – Yoga practice of sensory control and withdrawal

Puja – ritual offering, image worship

Purusha – inner person of pure consciousness

Raja Yoga – Yoga of mind and will, such as taught in *Yoga*

Sutras

Rajas – quality or guna of aggression and stimulation

Rigveda – oldest Veda and mantric source

Sadhana – Yoga and meditation practice or routine

Sakshi - witness

Samadhi – Yogic state of unity consciousness

Samana – balancing Prana

Sarasvati – Goddess of knowledge

Sat – pure being

Sattva – higher quality of balance, intelligence, virtue

Shakti – Cosmic power as a feminine principle

Shiva – Cosmic power of dissolution, transcendent consciousness

Siddha Yoga – Shaivite higher Yoga

Siddhi – yogic power or realization

Smriti – memory

Sushumna – central nadi or channel of subtle body

Sushupti – state of deep sleep

Svapna – state of dream

Tamas – quality of darkness and inertia

Tapas – power of inner fire, heat, transformation

Tarpaka Kapha – form of Kapha governing brain and nervous system

Turiya – fourth or transcendent state

Udana – ascending Prana

Upanishads – key texts of Vedanta and Self-inquiry

Vairagya – non-attachment, detachment

Vata – biological air humor or dosha

Vedanta – Vedic philosophy of Self-realization

Vedas – mantric texts of the Rishis

Vichara – meditative inquiry and investigation

Vijnana – experiential knowledge

Vikalpa – imagination

Vishnu – Cosmic force of sustenance and balance

Viveka – discrimination or discernment as a higher mental function

Vrittis – activities of the mind

Vyana – expanding Prana

Yajna – sacrifice, offering or giving as a principle of action

Yoga Nidra – yogic sleep or state of mergence

Yoga Sutras – key Yoga compilation of Patanjali Rishi

2. Sanskrit Pronunciation

For help with transliterated Sanskrit letters found in the text.

Note that we have only used these in the case of a few mantras, not for all Sanskrit terms. We have included only those few letters that are pronounced rather differently than their normal English equivalents, emphasizing the vowels which are most important.

a as in *a* book

ā as in f*a*ther

i as in *i*t

ī as in st*ea*m

u as in p*u*t

ū as in sh*oo*t

ṛ as in *ri*ver

e as in c*a*ke

ai as in f*i*re

o as in h*o*me

au as in h*ou*nd

c as in *ch*urch

ch as in i*tch*

ñ as in ca*ny*on

ś as in s*h*ip

ṣ as s*h*ut

ḥ soft h sound

3. Bibliography

Aurobindo, Sri. HYMNS TO THE MYSTIC FIRE. Twin Lakes, WI: Lotus Press, 2010.

Aurobindo, Sri. THE LIFE DIVINE. Twin Lakes, WI: Lotus Press, 2010.

Aurobindo, Sri. THE SYNTHESIS OF YOGA. Twin Lakes, WI: Lotus Press, 2010.

Chinmayananda, Swami, MANDUKYA UPANISAD WITH KARIKA. Mumbai, India: Central Chinmaya Mission Trust, 2011.

Chopra, Shambhavi. YOGINI: UNFOLDING THE GODDESS WITHIN. Delhi, India: Wisdom Tree Books, 2006.

Chopra, Shambhavi. YOGIC SECRETS OF THE DARK GODDESS. Delhi, India: Wisdom Tree Books, 2007.

COLLECTED WORKS OF VASISHTHA KAVYAKANTHA GANAPATI MUNI (Sanskrit only), twelve volumes, edited by K. Natesan. Tiruvannamalai, India: Sri Ramanasramam 2003–2007.

EIGHT UPANISHADS, WITH THE COMMENTARY OF SANKARA, by Swami Gambhirananda , Calcutta, India: Advaita Ashram 1972.

HATHA YOGA PRADIPIKA of Svatmarama. Adyar, India: Adyar Library and Research Centre, The Theosophical Society, 1972.

MAHABHARATA, INCLUDING BHAGAVAD GITA

Patanjali, *YOGA SUTRAS*. Varanasi, India: Bharatiya Vidya Prakashana, with commentaries of Vachaspati Mishra and Vijnana Bhikshu, 1983.

Bhagavan Ramana Maharshi, SADDARSHANA BHASHYA, Tiruvannamalai, India: Sri Ramanasramam, 1968.

RIGVEDA SAMHITA
COLLECTED WORDS OF SHANKARACHARYA

UPANISHADS, ONE HUNDRED AND EIGHTY EIGHT (Sanskrit only). Delhi, India: Motilal Banarsidass, 1980.

By the Author

Frawley, David, Kshirsagar, Suhas. ART AND SCIENCE OF VEDIC COUNSELING. Twin Lakes, WI: Lotus Press, 2016.

Frawley, David. INNER TANTRIC YOGA. Twin Lakes, WI: Lotus Press, 2008.

Frawley, David. MANTRA YOGA AND PRIMAL SOUND. Twin Lakes, WI: Lotus Press, 2010.

Frawley, David. RAMANA MAHARSHI'S ESSENCE OF SELF-REALIZATION. Goa, India: Vedic Wisdom Press, 2018.

Frawley, David. SOMA IN YOGA AND AYURVEDA. Twin Lakes, WI: Lotus Press, 2012.

Frawley, David. TANTRIC YOGA AND THE WISDOM GODDESSES. Twin Lakes, WI: Lotus Press, 1994.

Frawley, David. VEDANTIC MEDITATION. Berkeley CA: North Atlantic Press, 2001.

Frawley, David. VEDIC YOGA: THE PATH OF THE RISHI. Twin Lakes, WI: Lotus Press, 2014.

Frawley, David. YOGA AND AYURVEDA: SELF-HEALING AND SELF-REALIZATION. Twin Lakes, WI: Lotus Press, 1999.

Frawley, David. YOGA AND THE SACRED FIRE. Twin Lakes, WI: Lotus Press, 2004.

Frawley, David, Lad, Vasant. YOGA OF HERBS. Twin Lakes, WI: Lotus Press, 1986, 2002.

4. Resources

David Frawley (Vamadeva Shastri)

David Frawley (Vamadeva Shastri) is one of the most respected Vedic teachers (Vedacharyas) in the world today, whose range of study includes Ayurveda, Yoga, Vedanta, Vedic astrology and the ancient Vedas. He is the author of forty published books translated into twenty languages over the last several decades. He has worked with various Vedic and Hindu organizations throughout the world.

Frawley is a rare recipient of the Padma Bhushan Award, the third highest civilian award of the government of India, for his diverse work in the Vedic field. He has a D.Litt. From SVYASA (Swami Vivekananda Yoga Anusandhana Sansthana) the only deemed Yoga university in India, and a second D. Litt. from Avadh University (Ayodhya) in Uttar Pradesh. He was given a National Eminence Award as a Vedacharya from the South Indian Education Society (SIES) in Mumbai.

Frawley is one of the four main advisors of NAMA (National Ayurvedic Medical Association) in the United States, which has honored him as an Ayurvedic doctor. He has been an advisor and Master Educator to the Chopra center since it's founding. He has been a keynote speaker for the ministry of AYUSH India at several conferences. He is an advisor to a number of Ayurvedic schools and organizations worldwide. His books on Ayurveda are among the first published and remain among the most widely used in the field. He has addressed mind and consciousness of in several books on Yoga and Vedanta as well.

@drdavidfrawley Facebook - @davidfrawleyved, Twitter

American Institute of Vedic Studies

Frawley is the director of the American Institute of Vedic Studies (www.vedanet.com, @americanvedic Facebook), which is an on-line educational center for Vedic Studies for students throughout the world. His wife Yogini Shambhavi joins him for teaching programs and Yoga retreats, as well offering Vedic astrology consultations. The website hosts more than two hundred original articles by Frawley on Vedic studies and a variety of resources, including regular new postings.

The institute offers four on-line courses

1) Ayurvedic Healing foundation course in Ayurveda – Ayurvedic view of body and mind, constitution, disease and treatment, emphasizing herbal and life-style therapies, since 1988.

2) Yoga, Ayurveda, Mantra and Meditation foundation course – including Ayurveda and Raja Yoga, *Yoga Sutras* and Sanskrit mantras, Vedanta and consciousness, since 2004.

3) Integral Vedic Counseling foundation course – sharing educational and communication skills and Vedic life guidance relative to all Vedic fields, since 2017.

4) Ayurvedic Astrology foundation course in Vedic astrology – fundamentals of Vedic astrology from birth charts to Muhurta, with special emphasis on the astrology of healing through Ayurveda, since 1985.

5. Endnotes

1 *Yoga Sutras* I.2, citta vṛtti nirodhaḥ

2 *Yoga Sutras* I.12-13

3 *Yoga Sutras* I.38, svapna nidrājñānālambanam

4 Like the Dharma Megha Samadhi of the *Yoga Sutras* IV.29.

5 *Yoga Sutras* IV. Kaivalya Pada deals with this subject.

6 *Yoga Sutras* I.2

7 *Yoga Sutras* I.2

8 *Yoga Sutras* I.10

9 *Yoga Sutras* I.9

10 Prashna Upanishad III. Entire chapter deals with the pranas.

11 Brihadaranyaka Upanishad IV.3. 1-32 refers to the Seer as Advaita. This section of the Upanishad deserves study like the Mandukya Upanishad and is even more detailed in what it presents.

12 Mandukya Karika of Gaudapadacharya.

13 Mandukya Karika of Adi Shankara.

14 Satapatha Brahmana

15 Discussed in the Prashna Upanishad II with Prana as the supreme power operating all our faculties. Other Upanishads also discuss the primacy of Prana.

16 Brihadaranyaka Upanishad I.3.28

17 Brihadaranyaka Upanishad IV.3.9. Refers to the Earth as the waking state or this world and Heaven as the deep sleep state or the world beyond, with dream as their juncture.

18 *Yoga Sutras* I. 24-28.

19 Kalana in Sanskrit

20 *Yoga Sutras* I.3

21 Like the many Pratah Smarami or morning remembrance chants or stotras of Hinduism.

22 Note author's Yoga of Herbs with Dr. Vasant Lad

23 *Yoga Sutras* I.9

24 *Yoga Sutras* IV.1

25 Brihadaranyaka Upanishad IV.3.9. Refers to the Earth as the waking state or this world; the Heaven as the deep sleep state or the world beyond; and dream as their juncture.

26 Like Prakriti laya state in Samkhya philosophy and *Yoga Sutras*.

27 Waking is of the Annamaya kosha or food sheath, dream is of Pranamaya, Manomaya and Vijnanamaya koshas, depending upon the level of dreaming. Pranamaya dreams are largely energetic and instinctual in nature. Manomaya dreams are sensory and emotional. Vijnanamaya dreams connect to deeper insight and cross over into deep sleep type meditations.

28 Dhyana Bhumis

29 *Yoga Sutras* I.3. Tadā draṣṭuḥ svarūpe'vasthānam

30 *Yoga Sutras* I.4. vṛtti sārūpyam itaratra

31 Five vrittis in *Yoga Sutras* I.5.

32 Note the teachings of Ramana Maharshi in this regard, like Upadesha Saram.

33 Mundaka Upanishad II.2.3-4.

34 Note author's book Mantra Yoga and Primal Sound, page 129.

35 *Yoga Sutras* I.23

36 Pronounced as the article 'a as in 'a' book.

37 Short a as in "*a* book". Long a as in "f*a*ther".

38 The letter-U as in the word p*u*t.

39 Sound as in f*a*ther.

40 Sound as in sh*oo*t.

41 M-sound drawn within and nasalized

42 Rigveda I.1.1

43 Note author's book, Vedic Yoga: The Path of the Rishi, pps. 213-221.

44 Note author's book, Vedic Yoga: The Path of the Rishi, pps. 86-98.

45 Note author's book, Vedic Yoga: The Path of the Rishi, pps. 229-237.

46 Chandogya Upanishad III.11.3.

47 Note author's book, Shiva, the Lord of Yoga, pps. 82-88.

48 Note author's book, Inner Tantric Yoga, page 194.

49 Note author's book, Inner Tantric Yoga, page 193.

50 *Yoga Sutras* I.26.

51 *Yoga Sutras*, Pranava. I.27.

52 *Yoga Sutras* I.28.

53 *Yoga Sutras* II.33.

54 Hridaya dharana in Sanskrit.

6. Index

"*Yoga of Consciousness* is an authentic and lucid exposition of how to awaken our limitless potential by an experiential understanding of our true Self. Vamadeva Shastri (David Frawley), himself a yogi and teacher of the highest order, embodies in this volume the wisdom of India's ancient tradition of self-realization, especially as expounded in the *Mandukya Upanishad*.

His account is illumined by the insights of great contemporary masters such as Sri Aurobindo, Ramana Maharshi, Swami Rama Tirtha, and Ganapati Muni. Perhaps the most important spiritual lesson of this book is how to un-lock the mysteries of sleep (*nidra*) in order to awaken super-consciousness (*prajna*). All told a must-read modern manual on Hindu spirituality by one of its foremost living exponents."

Professor Makarand R. Paranjape, A.M., Ph.D.
Director, Indian Institute of Advanced Study (IIAS), Shimla

"David Frawley's new book *The Yoga of Consciousness* addresses the question of consciousness directly. He skillfully shows that consciousness is not the same as the contents of the mind, but rather the *w* that shines on things. With his brilliant insights on the difference between consciousness and awareness-states, Frawley delineates a profound Yoga of consciousness.

The book is more than philosophy or abstract teaching; its goal is to provide the practitioner with different techniques that are in complete consonance with each of the states that the Vedas speak of: waking, dreaming, deep sleep, and the fourth state which is transcendental."

Subhash Kak, Padma Sri, author *In Search of the Cradle of Civilization*
Regents Professor of Computer Science Department,
Oklahoma State University

"In this brilliant book David Frawley (Vamadeva Shas¬tri) explains with elegance how reality differs in dai¬ly states of consciousness and how the true purpose of Yoga is to discover your true liberated timeless im¬mortal Self and change your identity from your provisional personality to your universal essence."

Deepak Chopra MD, author *Metahuman*

David Frawley Titles

Yoga & Ayurveda:

Self-Healing and Self-Realization

David Frawley

360 pp pb • $19.95 • ISBN: 978-0-9149-5581-8

Applied together, Yoga and Ayurveda open pathways to optimal health, vitality and higher awareness. Yoga and Ayurveda reveals the secrets hidden in our body, breath, senses, mind and chakras, and provides transformational methods to unlock these inner powers. Learn how diet, herbs, asana, pranayama and mediation hold the key to whole-being improvement and life-changing growth. The first book of its kind published in the West, Yoga and Ayurveda remains a must-read for anyone exploring these topics.

"Once again, Dr. David Frawley demonstrates his ability to make timeless wisdom relevant for the modern person. His new book illustrates why I consider David to be a true Rishi - a knower of reality. Yoga and Ayurveda should be in the library of every serious student of Yoga and Vedic knowledge."

– Deepak Chopra, M.D.,

"Yoga and Ayurveda impels, guides and teaches us how to connect our earthly physicality with our soulful aspirations, in the process teaching us the inner art of controlling our subtle energies. The author, hailed by Indian thinkers as one of today's foremost scholars of Hindu wisdom, does this not by some new age mumbo-jumbo but by returning us to the cosmic insight of India's sages. Hinduism Today endorses Yoga and Ayurveda and knows that it will further the on-going Hindu renaissance by virtue of the lucid, well- explained teachings that it contains."

– Hinduism Today

"Through a skillful exploration of the inner dimensions of these two great sister sciences, Dr. David Frawley has performed a wonderful service to anyone seeking to restore wholeness in body, mind & spirit."

– Pandit Rajmani Tigunait, Spiritual Director Of The Himalayan Institute

---

These books are available at bookstores and natural food stores nationwide.

To order a copy directly visit **LotusPress.com**

For more information or other ways to order

e-mail: **lotuspress@lotuspress.com** or call 262-889-8561

Lotus Press is the publisher of a wide range of books in the field of alternative health, including Ayurveda, Chinese medicine, herbology, aromatherapy, Reiki and energetic healing modalities.

Ayurveda and the Mind

The Healing of Consciousness

David Frawley

356 pp • $19.95 • ISBN: 978-0-9149-5536-8

Ayurveda and the Mind is perhaps the first book published in the West that explores specifically the psychological aspect of this great system. The book explores how to heal our minds on all levels from the subconscious to the superconscious, along with the role of diet, impressions, mantra, meditation, yoga and many other methods to create wholeness.

"Ayurveda and the Mind addresses, with both sensitivity and lucidity, how to create wholeness in Body, Mind and Spirit. This book opens the door to a new energetic psychology that provides practical tools to integrate the many layers of life. Dr. Frawley has added another important volume to his many insightful books on Ayurveda and Vedic sciences."
– **Deepak Chopra M.D.**, Author of *Yogini, Unfolding the Goddess Within*

"In this book Dr. David Frawley presents an insightful Ayurvedic perspective on healing the mind and consciousness."
– **Dr. Vasant Lad**, Author of *The Science of Self Healing*

"This book is a valuable resource to students of Ayurveda, Yoga, Tantra and psychology. Dr Frawley has once again demonstrated his unique talent of digesting ancient Vedic knowledge and feeding us this understanding, which nourishes our body, mind and soul."
– **David Simon M.D.**, Medical Director, The Chopra Center for Well Being

---

"This is a marvelous overview of the psychological and therapeutic aspects of Ayurveda, which the author regards as the healing branch of yogic science."
– **Dr. Georg Feuerstein**, Author, Director, Yoga Research Center

---

The Yoga of Herbs

Ayurvedic Guide to Herbal Medicine

2nd Revised and Enlarged Edition

David Frawley & Dr. Vasant Lad
288 pp • $15.95 • ISBN: 978-0-9415-2424-7

For the first time, here is a detailed explanation and classification of herbs, using the ancient system of Ayurveda. More than 2 70 herbs are listed, with 108 herbs explained in detail. Included are many of the most commonly used western herbs with a profound Ayurvedic perspective. Important Chinese and special Ayurvedic herbs are introduced. Beautiful diagrams and charts, as well as detailed glossaries, appendices and index are included.

"Dr. Frawley and Dr. Lad have made a truly powerful contribution to alternative, natural health care by their creation of this important book. This book ... will serve not only to make Ayurvedic medicine of greater practical value to Westerners but, in fact, ultimately advance the whole system of Western herbalism forward into greater effectiveness. I think anyone interested in herbs should closely study this book whether their interests lie in Western herbology, traditional Chinese herbology or in Ayurvedic medicine."
– **Michael Tierra**, Author of *The Way of Herbs*

"This book is a fresh application of Ayurvedic principles to Western herbs. As such it stands as a landmark in the development of Western herbology, allowing a deeper blending of Eastern and Western herbology."
– **Paul Bergner**, East West Journal

"The Yoga of Herbs provides a fascinating and readable look at Ayurveda. This book acts as a key, unlocking the mysteries of Eastern philosophies and medical practices. One views the energies and actions of American herbs with a fresh perspective after reading this valuable, timeless volume. Highly recommended."
– **Stephen Foster**, Herbalist, Author

"At Last! A book on the ancient and fascinating system of Ayurvedic herbs ... written for the Western student or practitioner of herbs."
– **Mark Blumenthal**, Publisher, HerbalGram, Official Newsletter of the Herb Industry

---

David Frawley Titles

Inner Tantric Yoga

Working with the Universal Shakti: Secrets of Mantras, Deities, and Meditation

David Frawley

280 pp • $19.95 • ISBN: 978-0-9406-7650-3

Inner Tantric Yoga presents the deeper tradition of Tantra, its multidimensional vision of the Divine and its transformative practices of mantra and meditation that take us far beyond the outer models of how Tantra is usually presented today. The book can expand your horizons about masculine and feminine energies, Self and world, universe and the Absolute into a living experience of the Infinite and Eternal both within and around you.

"With Inner Tantric Yoga, David Frawley reminds us that we have, hidden within our own deeper awareness, wonderful Gods and Goddesses in embryo who have but one intention: to bring the sacred back into our lives."
– **Deepak Chopra and David Simon**, the Chopra Center for Wellbeing

"Vamadeva (Dr. Frawley) is a living rishi who guides his students to the fullest scope of yogic insight and realization. His boook weaves Tantra, Veda and Yoga, Shakti and Shiva, into a magnificent tapestry of wisdom, beauty and delight."
– **Shambhavi Chopra**, Author of *Yogini, Unfolding the Goddess Within*

"David Frawley continues to bring new understandings of the esoteric aspects of Tantra and Yoga. This work is invaluable for all seekers of yoga who would know it in it fullest context as a spiritual art and practice."
– **Mukunda Stiles**, Author of *Ayurvedic Yoga Therapy*

"David Frawley, Vamadeva Shastri, is the preeminent American-born authority on Hindu philosophy and scripture. Inner Tantric Yoga is a new jewel from Vamadeva's store of precious treasures, and a "must have" for serious students of Eastern mystical teachings and dedicated practitioners. It receives my highest recommendation."
– **Thomas Ashley-Farrand**, Author of *Healing Mantras and Shakti Mantras*

These books are available at bookstores and natural food stores nationwide.

To order a copy directly visit **LotusPress.com**

For more information or other ways to order

e-mail: **lotuspress@lotuspress.com** or call 262-889-8561

Lotus Press is the publisher of a wide range of books in the field of alternative health, including Ayurveda, Chinese medicine, herbology, aromatherapy, Reiki and energetic healing modalities.

David Frawley Titles

Soma in Yoga and Ayurveda

The Power of Rejuvenation and Immortality

David Frawley

392 pp • $19.95 • ISBN: 978-0-9406-7621-3

What is the secret of Soma, the legendary mystic drink of immortality, first lauded by India's ancient Vedic seers? Is Soma a single plant, a type of plants, a way of healing, a special intoxicant, or an inner elixir produced by Yoga and meditation?

Going back to the vision of the Vedic seers, David Frawley reveals the secret of Soma for body, mind and spirit, with its profound implications from diet and herbs to pranayama, mantra and meditation. His new analysis of Soma, reflecting forty years of study of Vedic texts, is practical, comprehensive and deeply insightful – so that you can bring the secret power of Soma into all aspects of your life and consciousness, and for the world as a whole.

"Vamadeva's tour of well-being, incisive and empirical, always comes back to us, to the goodness in our life. His understanding of the doshas and what each of us needs to find balance within and ward off disease is uncanny. This book's fundamental message reminded me of Abraham Lincoln's maxim: "In the end, it's not the years in your life that count. It's the life in your years." The difference is, Vamadeva teaches us how to put the Divine life into all our days and years."

– **Paramacharya Sadasivanatha Palaniswami**, Hinduism Today, Editor-in-Chief

---

"Soma in Yoga and Ayurveda weaves together with remarkable clarity rejuvenation of the body, revitalization of the mind, and awakening to the inherent immortality of the Spirit. The book reveals special healing secrets of Soma from the ancient Vedic rishis and yogis reflecting a profound vision and wide range of application that can transform both our individual lives and our collective culture. Vamadeva Shastri has provided one of the most important and original books on Yoga and Ayurveda in recent times that is bound to be studied for decades to come."

– **Deepak Chopra**, Author of *Reinventing the Body, Resurrecting the Soul: How to Create a New Self*